MW01076902

SHORTY

A Life in Sports

SHORTY

A Life in Sports

by David H. White, Jr.

Copyright © 2007 David H. White, Jr.

Printed in the United States of America by Vaughan Printing of Nashville, Tennessee.

ISBN 094435321-5

We would like to thank the following newspapers for granting permission to use photographs from their archives to make this book possible — The *Birmingham Post-Herald* and *The Birmingham News*.

Book Design by Bill Segrest, Jr.

If you are interested in using SHORTY — A Life in Sports
for fundraising purposes or for corporate gifts, please email us at
SpecialSales@BrookSport.com.

For Beth, Isabelle and Fairbanks. My Life.

TABLE OF CONTENTS

INTRODUCTION

It All Starts with Hard Work
The dictionary is the only place where success comes before work. Hard work is the price we must pay for success. I think you can accomplish anything if you're willing to pay the price.
— *Vince Lombardi*

A Life in Sports

My name is David H. White, Jr., and I am a sportswriter. This is a book of candid observations and personal reflections about a former Alabama high school football coach, George O. White, Jr., known to his many friends and colleagues as "Shorty."

Coach White and I happen to share the same surname, but there is no relation between us and I have no interest or reason for writing this book other than to honor a man of deep integrity, a man who I believe has added great value not only to the community of Birmingham but, in a more abstract, yet equally important way, to the world at large.

Through the example of Coach White's life I am reminded that strength, the kind of strength for which generations are remembered, can only be earned by men and women of integrity, who strive for excellence every day. Their values have been forged, like steel in a furnace, through countless daily tests of character and sacrifice.

I first met Coach White when he was head coach at Pleasant Grove in the fall of '91. I had just returned for good to Birmingham, Alabama, the town where I had been raised. In the late '70s, I was away at Episcopal High School in Virginia, in the early '80s, at Vanderbilt University in Tennessee, and in the late '80s, in North Carolina, where I was a reporter, first for a Durham newspaper and then for the University of North Carolina Alumni Magazine. Even though I visited Birmingham often over those years—on holidays and events with my family or catching an occasional Alabama football game with friends—the truth is I had been emotionally absent for almost a decade and a half.

Almost as soon as I returned home, I hired on as a sports reporter for *The Birmingham News*. One of my first games was Pleasant Grove versus Midfield, two small-but-proud, working-class communities in the heart of Alabama's steel industry, just south and west of downtown Birmingham.

Years of experience had taught me that a high school football game requires a good forty-five minutes to an hour before each game to talk to the coaches, grab a hamburger, and get situated in the press box before play starts. Old habits do die hard, and I arrived for the seven o'clock kickoff at my usual time of six p.m.

Making my way across the parking lot, I headed straight to a gate opening out onto the field and then casually strolled across a freshly chalked gridiron to the Pleasant Grove Spartans. The boys were in the middle of pre-game drills. Coach White, arms folded across his chest, stood close by, watching with intense concentration.

After a few minutes of looking on as they ran a few plays, I caught Coach White's attention and asked him how the night was shaping up. First, he complimented the opposition, pointing out the strength of their players and the quality of their coaching staff. Then, completely at ease, he shared with me in precise detail what he thought his team needed to do to win the game.

As we talked, I was amused to learn that, ironically, just as I had been away from Birmingham since the late 1970s, Coach White too had only recently made his way back to Birmingham. In fact, this fall season was the first time he had coached high school football since he left Banks High in '75.

Coach White fondly recalled those years. He told me how proud he was of his three state championships and fourteen seasons at Banks because they represented "great kids, a great staff, and a lot of hard work and discipline." I had heard enough about Coach White, of course, to know that with his name recognition and his resumé he could have coached anywhere in the city or the county. "West End, Ramsay, Woodlawn, Ensley, Phillips, Huffman...Everybody had good talent," White said. "It's what made competition so keen back then."

But the University of Alabama had called him to interview for a coaching position and, well, the University of Alabama is the University of Alabama. How could he pass up a coaching job with the University of Alabama during the halcyon years of Paul W. "Bear" Bryant? It would prove to be the correct move for him and his family.

How does one measure the full impact of a man's life? Although the Pleasant Grove Spartans didn't win the game against Midfield that night in 1991, they had played extremely hard for four quarters. It was a highly competitive game. Here was a man, a proven leader, who had gotten the very best out of his players and although this man's coaching ability was absolutely obvious on the field, the record would forever read a loss.

A few weeks later, back in my office, I set aside a morning and an afternoon to dig deeper into the facts of his life. Yes, Shorty White had long been considered a football legend by those who follow Alabama football. Yes, Shorty was a hard-nosed coach who emphasized discipline and strength. Yes, Shorty was handed the job of head coach while under the wing of his mentor Coach Jimmy Tarrant in '61 and held that position, winning three state championships. And in just a few quick years after he joined Bear Bryant's staff, the Crimson Tide pulled in two national championships.

Then, in '81, Coach White left football and coaching for a successful insurance business in Tuscaloosa. Every article or mention I came across about Coach White's coaching prowess was positive and laudatory. Perhaps there are a few of the more calloused sports pundits today who may attempt to downplay his career as being one of "short stature"— fourteen seasons at the helm as a head coach pales in comparison to some of his colleagues' life-time tenures—but any serious student or historian of the game will agree that Coach White was instrumental in elevating the performance level of football and athletics in this state. In the early '60s, he implemented a weight-training program for his players, at the time anything but traditional. In the late '60s and early '70s, he introduced cutting-edge college-level football tactics, such as the Veer option on offense and the use of three linebackers on defense.

The more I reflected on my Pleasant Grove interview with Coach White the more I realized that not only was I impressed with his deep knowledge of the game and his players—which was, not surprisingly, considerable—but what struck me most was his extraordinary patience with my questions and his passion for the game. Coach White seemed honestly happy every minute of our conversation. Here was a consummate professional and you could tell he loved what he was doing.

His gracious humility and pleasant humor made my transition back to Alabama all the more welcoming. It felt good to be home. I made a note to get back to him at my earliest opportunity. He was unlike any other coach I had met at that point in my career.

I'm ashamed to admit that it took almost fifteen more years to follow up on that objective. In mid-2005, I was presented with a short piece on an Alabama high school football classic, the 1974 match-up between archrivals Banks and Woodlawn at Legion Field. "In the fall of 1974, forty-two thousand fans came to ... see the top two high school teams in the state compete for the region championship. The winner would most assuredly be the favorite to win the state 4A title," wrote Darryl White, the youngest of Coach White's three children. "It would be the largest crowd to ever see a high school football game in Alabama history. And over three decades later, the 1974 record attendance still stands."

Reading these words of introduction to that game—a son's homage to his father—I felt compelled to revisit the life of Shorty. As a sportswriter, I wanted to get my hands around the key distinguishing traits and characteristics that had helped him secure his reputation as one of Alabama's truly outstanding sports figures. I wanted to understand this man.

I gave Coach White a call. Several weeks later I interviewed him at his home in Helena, Alabama, and I decided to write this book.

I grew up in a Birmingham steel family. My father, who left the family business to teach history at the University of Alabama in Birmingham, taught me that any work is good work but that doing "good works" is perhaps the hardest work of all. It would take the example of Coach White's life to help me grasp the full reach and significance of my father's instruction.

Certainly, there have been and still are any number of "hard-working" coaches and dedicated football players in Alabama high school sports. A contemporary and somewhat notorious example, perhaps, can be seen in the career of Rush Propst of Hoover High School outside Birmingham. Propst often tells the press just how hard his team works—and the results on the scoreboard do indeed seem to substantiate that claim.

We all recognize, however, that the twin concepts of "hard work" and "winning"—like "wealth" and "riches," or "knowledge" and "information"—can prove to be misleading. Sometimes they just don't fit together neatly, hand in glove.

At the Pleasant Grove versus Midfield game that night, I remember how Coach White represented for me the epitome of class and unpretentious dignity required of a fine high school football coach. His calm and controlled demeanor convinced me that he was a man absolutely committed and dedicated to improving the character of young men's lives and not just to "winning" for the sake of "winning."

In the course of my research, I found that many of the players and coaches who knew him, or who had played against him, held the firm opinion that he was, without doubt, the hardest-working and the toughest football coach they had ever known. When I challenged him about his reputation for hard work, Coach White didn't bring up his three state championships or his fourteen years of having fielded solid, highly competitive football teams. Nor did he crow about his years at the University of Alabama and the two national championships under Bear Bryant.

No, Coach White simply explained to me that the lives and the actions of the young men he had coached and who now have moved on to become productive and hard-working citizens, would have to speak for him. To these men, he was coach, he was mentor, he was friend. "Their opinion matters, mine doesn't," he said.

Coach White did go on to say, however, that when he started coaching he recognized that he didn't have the knowledge that many other coaches had so he determined he would simply have to work harder than his counterparts. "My greatest asset," he said, "is that I value education. I know when I don't know something and I act quickly to find the right person to teach me what I need to know."

Coach White said he viewed each young athlete as a future businessman, teacher, principal, lawyer, minister, coach. "A good high school football coach has to be a teacher, first and foremost. Your job is to leave your mark not just on the scoreboard but on the quality of the choices your boys will make every day for the rest of their lives."

When I mentioned to Coach White that many sports commentators express the opinion that Rush Propst will surpass every other Alabama high school coach in the record books, Coach White responded by saying that "winning alone" is never proof that a team has worked harder than another team or that a coach has done his job. "Forget about the other guy. You can only know whether you've worked hard or not. Get all your priorities straight and in order, then check 'em off. That's the hardest work there is."

Perhaps, then, this is what my father was talking about when he spoke about "the hardest work of all."

Acting fair and square on the playing field, while making real sacrifices in the classroom, at home, and in the community each and every day adds a dimension to work that compounds its difficulties. When we win in one dimension of our lives without winning in others, we feel a loss and we feel diminished.

A life in sports and physical competition, whether it is an amateur's joy or a professional's occupation, does indeed hold out promise to live up to the ideal of doing "good works." At its very best, physical education has the potential to create foundations of hard work and sacrifice, of generosity and good will for young athletes. That is the productive legacy that tough-minded men like my father and Coach White have worked hard to pass on to new generations.

CHAPTER 1
Early Years (1931-1941)

George "Shorty" White was born in Baptist-Princeton Hospital in Birmingham on February 4, 1931, the son of Ruth Maxine Limbaugh White and George White, Sr. His infant years were spent in the Bush Hills community of Birmingham. His parents moved to the Woodlawn area because his father was mad at one of his brothers in the trucking business. White was five. One of White's fondest memories of the Woodlawn area was going to Polar Bears, an ice cream store, where he would get a couple of scoops of his favorite ice cream when he had the money to afford it.

White remembers trying to cross the street in Woodlawn when he was around eight years old and almost being hit by a car. "I couldn't read the signs, it scared me to death. There was usually hardly any traffic on that street. My mother picked me up from school and she was very worried about me. I check those lights now."

His mom's family gatherings at his grandparents' farm houses were on the way to Atlanta down I-20. His dad's family had a farm and they had a lot of horses and cattle. White loved riding horses. "The one I rode was very tame and easy to handle."

White remembers when he was ten getting his hand stuck in the washing machine and cousin Robert Thornton reversing the machine so White wouldn't have his hand shredded.

White also remembers riding around in the car with George Sr., his dad, and George Sr. singing songs in the car. "He had a good voice," White says. "Those were pleasant times with him."

Shorty also remembers the hard times when his father drank and was abusive mentally and physically to his mother. "He could be the nicest guy to be around when he was sober but when he drank he was just mean. I remember Uncle Jim, Ruth's brother, coming over and he and my dad getting in a brawl. Uncle Jim ran him off and told him to not come back."

White says that losing his dad from divorce was difficult though many times he couldn't stand to be around him.

"I felt like I had been cheated," he says. "It makes you angry. I was unhappy about it. Most kids develop a friendship with both parents. I feel like it had a lot to do with my academic performance. Adults today know the importance of taking kids and educating them and they continue that on a daily basis. I had a lot more intelligence in school than I realized and I learned that later in life. I just didn't get a good start at it."

White decided when his mom remarried, to Lewis Peyton Sidle, in 1940 and the family moved to Elyton Village that he was going to excel at something. "Mature people work to reach their goals. Mine was sports. When my parents, Lewis and Ruth, moved to Elyton Village that was the best move we ever made."

White remembers going to games with Lewis at Legion Field and watching the big schools in the city, Woodlawn, Ensley, Phillips, Ramsay and West End—the big 5—play. He loved the game.

One other fond memory for White was watching Lewis play fast-pitch softball. According to White, Lewis was a fine pitcher and his Navy team won the South Pacific Championship over all other teams in the islands during the War. Robert Owen, who helped White out with his paper route, was Lewis's catcher.

White remembers playing football with the older kids in the Village. "I wasn't scared to get hurt. I got my nose broken one time, but I kept on playing."

Gone With the Wind was a huge hit in 1939 and White remembers there was a movie with Walter Pidgeon that he enjoyed. It was about a German invasion of England in WWII and how the Germans pushed the British back. It portrayed one of the worst defeats of the war.

White always comes back to Ruth, "my hero."

"She was such a good person. She was too easy on me. She really let me get away with too much. If I needed something she'd get it for me. She'd always find a way to get the money to buy it for me. The most amazing thing was how she survived with no more money coming in than she had. We were always fed well, we had nice clothes and we had money on the weekend to go to the Mickey Mouse Club for a dime or to the Royal Theater and see a double feature and buy a candy bar, hot dog and an RC Cola for 50 cents."

White would also work himself, to make some extra money, cutting grass at the Village. He'd sign out a push mower and cut yards for 10 cents a yard so he could make enough money for the weekends.

In 1942, Lewis went off to war; he was stationed in San Francisco, Hawaii, and Guam, where he perished in 1945. Lewis's father was a big man and that's where White's brother Jimmy, Lewis and Ruth's son, got his size from. Jimmy was 6-3, 225 pounds and according to White, "could play by today's standards."

White says that Lewis was a great guy who loved his mother unconditionally; he also took a keen interest in Shorty and loved him and his brother equally.

The Whites would go to different churches when they were younger. There was the First Methodist Church in Ensley and the Irondale First Baptist Church. There was a small church outside the Village that they attended also. They didn't have transportation, as his mother never had a car until White was in college, so getting places required walking. That was not a problem for White.

White remembers when he and Lewis spent their last time together before Lewis went off to war. "He told me, 'You're the man of the house—take care of your mother and Jimmy.'" Jimmy was two years old.

"I remember going upstairs to get Jimmy out of his room and coming down the stairs with him in my arms when Jimmy was real little. The stairs were concrete and I was wearing no shoes or socks and cuffed pants—and I tripped down the stairs and bruised myself up. I cradled Jimmy when I was falling and somehow, by the way I held him, he didn't have a scratch. We were lucky."

White says that Jimmy never had a man around the house to discipline him though Lewis was a disciplinarian. Jimmy was maybe a little indulged by his mother but according to Shorty he was a "sweet, good-hearted guy."

One of Shorty's major regrets is that his mother wasn't able to meet his wife June. "June reminds me a lot of her. The Lord sent June my way. She reminds me of my mother in the way she manages money so well, she's a bargain shopper and just a good Christian gal. I am very fortunate."

His mother, through her strength of character, always found a way to provide for him and Jimmy.

"Women have a real instinct to work things out," Shorty says. "They're better at it than men. To have not had more than an elementary school education, she had a ton of common sense. When she was growing up the children would work on the farm. I wish she had seen me get a college degree and a Masters and seen what I did in athletics. That would have thrilled her to death.

"She was a special person who had so many disappointments in her life. Her first husband was a wife abuser. Her second husband was a straight-up guy, killed in the war. It was enough to knock the foundation out from under you. But she had a very strong constitution. She refused to accept defeat." In athletic terms, she found a way to win.

White loved his mother unabashedly, not only for her selflessness, but also as a boy and as a son, because she was "a loving sweet woman."

"She was sweet, soft-spoken, just a good lady. We had food, water and clothes. We didn't have much else. Vacations were out of the question. But she always fed us and I was never embarrassed with what I wore. How she did it, I will never know."

Ruth would work jobs at Merita Bakery and save enough from that, Social Security, and a military pension to take care of her young sons, keeping them well fed and able to attend school and play sports and be with friends.

"She gave her sons everything she had and then some." She was Shorty's world along with his friends and his athletics.

Shorty's father, George Sr., was an electrician and photographer and worked for his brother Bradley's trucking business. "He could do almost anything."

There were seven White brothers and Bradley was the oldest. They were all in the moving business in Birmingham at the time. Shorty remembers Bradley as difficult.

"He didn't treat people right, even his own brothers."

Shorty says that his dad was well spoken though he did not have a high school education. "I'm not even sure if he graduated from elementary school. But he was smart—he could do almost anything." He moved out to Los Angeles (after the divorce from Shorty's mother) as an electrician. "He thought he could make more money out there."

His dad saw one football game that he played in. "He probably sat by himself or with Uncle Bradley."

The final time Shorty remembers spending time with his dad was when he was in the military at Fort Jackson in South Carolina. His dad came to see him. He called to say he was coming, came to the post and drove up "Tank Hill" in his truck. Shorty doesn't recall it as a memorable visit and a few months later his father died in a fire caused by his smoking in the back of a truck warehouse where he spent the night before leaving the next morning.

"He got confused and went out the back instead of the front and the smoke killed him. I went to the funeral. He had gotten remarried and as far as I know it went fine."

George Sr. and his second wife had a son, Mark. Shorty spends time with him today.

"We'll meet on Saturdays with him and his wife, Joanie. He'll come over and watch football with me sometimes."

Shorty had an empty feeling of not having a male figure at home when he was young. He and his mom had to raise his younger brother Jimmy. That was a lot to ask of a pre-teen, having to grow up quickly.

When his mother died in 1952, Shorty remembers Coach Jimmy Tarrant, his high school football coach at Phillips, and Coach Ernie Tucker, his track coach, coming by to see him and offering their sympathies.

"I questioned myself whether I wanted to get a college degree," White remembers. "After that visit from my two coaches, I decided if I ever got a college degree I wanted to be a coach. My coaches influenced my life."

The first school Shorty can remember attending was an elementary school in Woodlawn near Woodlawn High School.

"I was not a good student," he recalls. "It was never encouraged at home. My mom cared about my schooling but I was never read to, which is so important."

It was all about the work ethic and doing the right thing in life at the White house. Ruth gave Shorty all she had financially and emotionally, but she had only an elementary school education so academics was not emphasized. Shorty says that changed later when he got to college and realized he needed a degree to pursue a successful professional life.

And there was always athletics; he excelled at the track meets and football.

Shorty came to love Lewis unconditionally. Lewis convinced Shorty to attend Phillips High School, where Lewis had gone. "He told me that it was the best school in the city and in the state. We lived in the Village and I had wanted to go to Woodlawn. I made the right decision. I went there in eighth grade."

Shorty says that Lewis had gone out for football when he had played at Phillips and had his front teeth knocked out. Lewis's father did not let him play for that reason, but Lewis wanted Shorty to play.

Shorty remembers Lewis taking him to the barbershop one day and telling the barber to give him a crew cut. Then Lewis got one himself.

"We got home and we caught it from my mother. We were two skin heads."

Lewis was a Navy Seabee in World War II. In April of 1945 in Guam, he was dropping dynamite to create some more depth in the bay to clear the way for carriers to dock in the bay. "They were rolling barriers, depth chargers," Shorty recalls. "And somebody got careless and blew 'em up."

It was devastating for Ruth and Shorty and young Jimmy, who was probably unaware at the time.

"We had to start over without him. I was becoming a teen. I loved him like he was my dad. My mother had it so hard. I lost my father. I miss him to this day."

It's a painful memory for the coach even today. Lewis was such a kind and gentle man and loved Ruth and the boys so much and took care of them. He was going to give them the quality of life that they deserved.

"My mother was hysterical, normal when you lose a loved one. I wanted to change my last name to Sidle, and if he had come home, I would have."

Shorty and his mom had to persevere and raise Jimmy.

When Shorty got the news he knew of only one thing to do.

"I remember I went upstairs in the front bedroom and got by the big window and got on my knees and started praying that it really wasn't true. It broke my heart. Not only mine, but my mother's and Jimmy's. Jimmy never got to know his dad and that was so sad."

The coach paused to reflect and allow himself to cry and think of the man who had meant everything to him, his mother and Jimmy. It was a poignant moment that brought back some painful, sad memories. It was Shorty and Jimmy's chance to have a father they could count on, a man with values and morals. And it was a chance for their mom to have some personal happiness.

"Before Jimmy's death, he did go to Hawaii where my father was buried. Jimmy was probably two years old when it happened. He was just a baby. You can't believe how it affected us. We had uncles on my mother's side. Uncle Jim lived in Central City and they got us to move close to them. They helped us out financially."

Elyton Village was a nice group of apartments built by the government for families with husbands/fathers in the military. They were reasonable to rent and though the inhabitants were not wealthy, they were close-knit. It was a solid community.

"It was all we could afford. Those were scary times," Shorty remembers.

Shorty remembers the address: 406 1st Street West. There was one family of five paratroopers who all came back alive from the war. Shorty remembers a man who lived seven doors down from him being shot in the back "but it didn't kill him." A man next door was shot in the head. "Then we got ours."

Shorty was crazy about Jimmy—born in 1942—and looked after

him. Jimmy lived with Shorty and June and went on to play for Coach Jimmy Tarrant at Banks. Jimmy was a stellar football player and one of the best athletes Shorty has ever seen. Jimmy was so good at Auburn that he landed on the cover of *Sports Illustrated* in 1964 in an issue titled, "The Year of the Running Back."

Shorty as well always excelled in sports; he was a superior athlete who had the speed, strength and endurance along with an unyielding determination to succeed on a high level in athletics. He and his friends would play tackle football when they were in elementary school on pavement and bruise each other up. There was no question of Shorty's tenacity. He was toughness personified.

While Shorty was cranking out the yards as a running back on the football team and starring in track, he also tried to play basketball. He was playing early in high school and one of his teammates had the ball stolen from him. The opponent was heading down the court and Shorty catapulted him into the fourth row of the seats when the player tried to go in for a lay-up. "My coach, Coach Tucker said, 'You can't do that, this is not football.' I said, 'he didn't score.' Basketball wasn't for me. I was a contact guy."

Shorty looked for another sport that would grab his attention, one that he could also shine at. It was boxing. He trained at the Birmingham Boys Club.

Shorty loved boxing and would passionately pursue it in middle school and high school. Shorty remembers "Fight Night." The kids in the neighborhood would listen to the fights on the radio. Jake LaMotta would fight Billy Conn in the middleweight division and Joe Louis would fight Max Schmeling, a German, in the heavyweight division. "We'd go to College Hills some nights and listen to it. They were wealthier than we were but it didn't matter."

Shorty started getting into his competitive mode when he was eight years old. "I was interested in anything real competitive. I got excited about it."

Competitiveness runs in the White family. His half-brother, Mark White, is proof of this. Shorty and Mark's father was George O. White, Sr., who took care of Mark until George's death in 1955. Shorty White did not have a good relationship with his father but Mark calls his father "my buddy. I loved him very much." He was born in 1944 in Los Angeles and moved back south with his father when his mother died right before Christmas of 1948.

Mark is proud of what his brother accomplished as an athlete and as a coach. Mark said that Shorty got him involved in some investments when his older brother was in the business and the investments have been "very profitable."

Mark worked in real estate, then in rehabilitation work and finally as a security guard. He draws retirement and Social Security now and may go back to work if he finds the right job. His wife since 1986, Joanie, is a registered nurse and clinic manager of Fresenius Medical Center, the largest dialysis center in the country.

Mark was Mr. Birmingham, Mr. North Alabama and Mr. Alabama in 1976. He was a dedicated champion bodybuilder. He also finished second in Chattanooga and in Northwest Florida in competitions he thought he had won. He got to know Arnold Schwarzenegger, the famous bodybuilder, actor and now governor of California in the late 70's; Mark met Schwarzenegger when he was appearing in *Stay Hungry*, filmed in Birmingham. He worked out with Mark at one of his gyms. They stayed in touch for some years. Mark got out of bodybuilding in 1981 when he saw steroids making a negative impact on the sport.

Mark calls himself "rebellious" after his father died and Shorty helped look after him. After their father's funeral, Shorty took Mark to Waite's in Southside Birmingham for lunch, put his arm around his younger brother, and promised to give him support.

Mark got to work and later settled down. He has made a good life for himself and Joanie.

He adds that White has raised very successful children and "he's a good man. He's going to heaven for sure."

CHAPTER 2
Wartime (1941-1945)

World War II was a time of great patriotism and great fear amongst most Americans, and residents of Birmingham, Alabama were no different. Shorty White was busy with so many activities that there was hardly any time for school.

"People didn't stress reading and getting an education like they do today," he observes. "Most of our parents didn't have a college education and many of them didn't have a high school education. There was patriotism though. It was the greatest generation who made the greatest contribution to our country."

Shorty remembers the first and only time he skipped school. His principal at Graymont Elementary was Captain Fred Kelly. Shorty describes him as "a good man." He went over to Shorty's house and Ruth said the boy wasn't there. So he went over to Frank Garner's house—he was also not at school—and caught the boys. Young Shorty was put to work cutting grass, weeding and picking up rocks on the playground. That was the only school day he ever missed.

His recreation included going to Legion Field and climbing the back wall to get in for high school football games. He and his friends would scale the wall and run into the stadium. Shorty said that the policeman could only catch one of them and he usually let all them in. Shorty would watch high school football—which he came to have a passion for—the city track meets, and the marching bands.

He found other ways to get into the Old Gray Lady. He would sell *The Birmingham News* outside the stadium. He would be able to go in and watch the college games after he had sold the load of papers he was assigned to sell. "Getting in the games was my payday there."

He would also sell programs and make a little money doing that and get to see the games. Football was definitely a passion for this active young man.

"Reading was not emphasized as much in some families. Kids could not afford to go to college. Once they got out of high school, they had to go to work. Then they got married and raised a family."

Shorty walked to school. "We didn't have a car. People today are lazy and fat and drive everywhere. We would walk and hitchhike to school and think nothing of it."

There was no television then for Shorty; he grew up listening to the radio. Shorty remembers listening to it when Pearl Harbor was attacked but "not having a thorough understanding of what was fixing to take place in the country. It was a trying time for an awful lot of people."

Shorty remembers five brothers who lived five doors down from him who were in the airborne armed services who jumped out of planes. Shorty believes there was probably a 15-20 percent chance of surviving jumps out of planes in Europe. Germans would shoot the men down in the air. Extraordinarily, all five brothers returned home.

Shorty was busy working and having fun with his friends. "There were so many activities. We did a lot better stuff than they do today."

But Shorty also had that work ethic ingrained in him from his stepfather Lewis and his mother.

He inherited a newspaper route from Robert and Mimi Owen. Robert was a merchant marine who helped haul supplies over to Russia during the war since Russia had the manpower but not the machine power. The U.S. would ship tanks, ammunition, planes, anything the Russkies needed for supplies. The Germans eventually picked up on it and started sinking American vessels. "There's no telling how many they sank," White remembers. "We were supplying them while we were building ourselves. That was the greatest contribution from America of any generation. Everybody came together. What is it that the Japanese admiral (Yamamoto) said, 'I'm afraid we've awakened a sleeping giant.' That was after the attack on Pearl Harbor."

Shorty would spend the night with Robert and Mimi on Saturday nights and get up at 2 a.m. on Sundays to stuff papers. Then he'd run the route with them. "Many people were too busy working, they couldn't afford college," he recalls. "These parents would have been excellent students if they had been given the opportunity."

Shorty recalls that the U.S. Congress was united in its war efforts. "There was no bickering like there is today. The Congress came together and stayed together until the problem was solved."

In each classroom there was an opportunity to contribute to the war effort. Shorty remembers buying 10-cent stamps while a classmate,

Carolyn Adams, bought $25 dollar war bonds. "Her dad owned a grocery store and a coal yard."

Shorty's stepdad Lewis went to war in 1942. He had bad ulcers, and could have opted to stay out of combat but felt it was his duty to go to battle for his country.

Shorty was doing other odd jobs like cutting grass with mowers that didn't have motors in them. "The motor was you," he says.

He got his second bike from George Owen, who played football for Wake Forest and was a native of the Village. It was a Schwinn. "I wanted that thing so bad," Shorty says. "I loved that bike."

He and a friend hitchhiked to see George play in the Blue-Gray game in Montgomery. Shorty recalls that George was a "giant" then. He was 6 feet tall, well over 200 pounds. He became an outstanding football coach in Florida later.

Shorty and his group of friends went to a sandwich shop after the game. They pointed to the owner that the guy in the back would pay and they ran all the way to the highway. "We didn't want to break the law, we were just hungry."

Shorty remembers listening to the radio program The Shadow, a popular mystery. His mom would sip tea outside with friends during the war. He and his buddies would go to the pro wrestling matches on Monday nights. There was a wrestler named Sailor Watkins who Shorty notes, "had cauliflower ears."

"I went up to him after a match and asked him if I could feel one of his ears. He was a scary guy. I barely touched one of his ears and he went 'Yoww!!!!' I nearly jumped out of my skin."

Shorty would also go to Lowe's skating rink and watch the pretty girls. He and his friends would walk and hitchhike from Elyton to 5 Points West. They'd also walk or hitchhike to Rickwood Field.

Watching Lucky Teeter was a favorite pastime of Shorty's. He would drive cars and make daring jumps over a group of vehicles, as a predecessor to Evel Knievel, the daredevil of the 1960's and 70's. Shorty remembers Teeter driving swiftly around the Legion Field track with one hand out the window waving to the crowd. He'd accelerate to the ramp in his car, hit the ramp and fly over cars lined up side by side. "It was better entertainment than they had today," White says. "He got killed at the beginning of the war doing his last jump. He rammed into another car."

Shorty was having too much fun to worry about school.

One time he got home late from a night at Legion Field with an intense pain in his side. His mother told him he better not be faking to miss school. She called Uncle Jim and he took Shorty to the hospital. They took out his appendix. "It could have ruptured if we had waited ten more minutes," Shorty recalls.

Shorty remembers traveling with Lewis when he went off to the war. Lewis left from the Terminal Station in Birmingham, a quaint railroad building that Shorty insists should have been kept up as a museum today. When Lewis told Shorty he had to be the man of the house and take care of his momma and Jimmy, Shorty cried.

Lewis would frequently write Ruth from overseas and tell her how things were going and that he missed her, Shorty and Butch, Jimmy's nickname at the time. Lewis frequently called Ruth "honey" and baby" in the letters.

When they got word of Lewis's death May 5, 1945, Shorty heard his mother scream. Shorty ran up to his mother's room, got on his knees and started praying. "It took me awhile to accept him because of my first experience with my dad, but I was going to change my name when he got home. He was such a good man and so good to my mother. I prayed that it wasn't true. I was so tired of getting kicked in the teeth and was praying for help for my mother, Jimmy and me."

To White, life was difficult during wartime but the unity of all Americans was unprecedented and may never be duplicated. It was a tremendous challenge for Americans, the leaders and the people of this country, with two enemies in two parts of the world determined to conquer the world.

The Germans led by the tyrannical Adolph Hitler had conquered much of Europe and were not going to stop until they Nazified the world. The Japanese were just as imperialistic and opened the Asian theater of war when they attacked and killed thousands of Americans in Pearl Harbor.

It was a dangerous time in the history of this country, but White remembers how united the people were from the smallest towns to the largest cities.

Many people sacrificed.

"It was all about duty and honor," White says. "I don't recall anything said about being defeated. That was out of the question. We didn't know how long it would take. That it was finished in less than five years is amazing. There was no division between Republicans and Democrats. Everybody came together in the smallest towns in the country. Everybody made sacrifices."

Women were performing duties usually reserved for men; with a lack of males in the country women were building tanks, ships and airplanes and also caring for the wounded.

"The amazing part about it was that most of the men were volunteers. There was never a more patriotic time than the 40's. Korea, Vietnam, Iraq not even World War I compares. The only thing that compares to it is the Civil War." The strong work ethic instilled in these young men would propel them the rest of their lives.

White was busy raising his little brother. Jimmy was as rambunctious as a wolf in a cattle barn. He was a good kid but he was loaded with energy and always getting into accidents. One time he climbed a tree and fell off when the limb broke and busted his nose open on a bench below. White thought he was dead. He fell off a coal bin one time and hurt himself only to recover and later get his leg run over by a pickup truck. There were no broken bones.

Jimmy had natural ability in athletics and White developed it. White would work diligently with Sidle in track in ninth and tenth grade. "I knew he was going to be a good athlete." Dewell Crumpton later coached Jimmy to a state championship in the hurdles.

Sidle was 6-3, 225 pounds, built like a modern-day quarterback. He played at Banks for Coach Tarrant and earned a scholarship to Auburn. Though Sidle graced that cover of *Sports Illustrated* in 1964 as a running quarterback for Auburn, he struggled with injuries because White says he never applied himself to weight training. A fierce competitor, he loved to play pickup basketball and other competitive sports. Sidle did get drafted by the Dallas Cowboys and played running back, as a starter, then went to the Atlanta Falcons before finishing with British Columbia in the Canadian Football League. Injuries prevented him from excelling to the fullest in college and the pros.

"If we could have combined his talent with my work ethic, it would have been awesome," White says.

CHAPTER 3
High School Stardom (1946-1950)

Coach Jimmy Tarrant, formerly of Phillips High School in Birmingham, describes White as a player who had "more guts than Jesse James." Tarrant thought White's courage along with his superb athletic ability made him one of the better players in the city at a time when city football was the best in the state. "He had so much integrity for the game. He wanted to be a success and had the discipline to be a success."

Tarrant coached White in the 1950 Clinic game against Woodlawn. "He had a great game. He averaged about 50 yards a punt and kicked one 80 yards in that game." Phillips had beaten Woodlawn two weeks earlier 20-19, but in this game with White running for two scores along with Tarrant's excellent defensive game plan, Phillips shut out the Colonels of Woodlawn 20-0. The game, played at Legion Field, drew 38,000 people and set the record for attendance at an Alabama high school football game that was broken in 1974 when White coached Banks against Woodlawn. That game drew 42,000.

Tarrant had played at Howard University (now Samford) then went up to Tennessee and competed in a spring training, winning a starting spot at tailback. He was ruled ineligible to play in the fall after his first spring; the SEC athletic directors voted against his transfer from Howard to Tennessee because they did not want him to play at Tennessee against their schools. The talented Tarrant posed a one-man threat to their schools' won-loss record. He practiced the next year in the spring, but was called to Fort Benning in the fall for military service in 1944. Tarrant served in the Army as a paratrooper for two years, then went into the NFL and was the starting quarterback for the Miami Seahawks. He tore up his groin and was let go during the middle of the season. From there he went to Phillips and started his high school coaching career in 1947.

He led the Red Raiders to the state championship in 1950, White's senior year.

Tarrant also coached White's brother, Jimmy Sidle, at Banks in 1960.

"They were both great competitors and I admired them both," Tarrant said. "Jimmy probably had more athletic talent than Shorty, but Shorty was a combative little rascal. I think Shorty could have been a great punt returner and runner at Auburn. I think he got disgusted that he didn't get to play down there."

Tarrant was an innovator who used the passing game and various formations with gadget plays like designing the center eligible play for the pass. He also had a great defensive mind as he set the defense that shut out Woodlawn in the 1950 Clinic game that featured the two best teams in the city. His 1950 team was special.

"I couldn't believe the year," he says. "*The Birmingham News* and *Post-Herald* voted us state champion. *The Montgomery Advertiser* voted Etowah state champions, but we played 'em the next year and beat 'em."

As a coach, Tarrant says that White was just as fierce on the sidelines.

"He was very aggressive and covered all the fundamentals. He was hard-nosed. He wouldn't tolerate any student breaking the rules. It didn't take much for Shorty to kick a player off the team. He kicked a player off the team when he heard about him drinking even though he was one of his best players. He ran a well-disciplined team. Every good football team is well-disciplined."

White is proud that Jimmy Tarrant treated him and Dewell Crumpton—his two assistant coaches on the Banks staff from '59-'61—like his players. There was no playing favorites when it came to disciplining his players or his coaches.

"One time Dewell and I may have been five minutes late to a meeting and Coach Tarrant paddled us. We weren't late anymore."

Like White, Tarrant was an innovator in offensive football, well ahead of his time. Tarrant used the Wing T, an offense that has stood the test of time, used in high school football today. Tarrant also spread it out on offense using five wide receivers at a time.

White says that one time Tarrant gave him and Crumpton a playbook that they studied diligently to get ready for the season. "We broke it down, we were excited about it. Then he threw it out the first day of practice."

Tarrant was a genius at offensive play-calling and what White learned about coaching came a lot from Tarrant, who had three outstanding players on the '60 team, White's second year at Banks: Jimmy Sidle, White's younger brother, George Morris and Larry Camp were the horses. There were some other good ones, Jimmy Mikul, Gary Seilacher and Jerry Popwell. The rest of the team had average talent. The Jets had lost to Ensley in the regular season but "tore 'em up" in the Clinic game, White says. They finished 5-4-1. It was a major improvement from the '59 season when the Jets finished 1-1-6. "We were a team under construction. Coach Tarrant and I had our disagreements." Shorty remembers. "We'd argue all the time and he usually won." Sidle went on to Auburn to play ball and Camp and Morris went to Georgia Tech. White calls the '60 team, "a great bunch of kids."

White also played for Tarrant and remembers that special '50 season when the Phillips Red Raiders led by White completed a perfect 10-0 season capped by the 20-0 win over Woodlawn in front of 38,000 fans at Legion Field. White remembers scoring two touchdowns in that game, the Crippled Children's Classic game. He also remembers fumbling twice.

"I did not fumble a lot in my playing career," he says. "I had two fumbles and two touchdowns."

White had a TD run in the game and caught a touchdown pass from quarterback Bobby Duke for the other score. Phillips had only beaten Woodlawn by a point in their regular season meeting, but in the Crippled Children's game White and his teammates dominated.

White loved working for Tarrant but his unyielding goal was to become a head football coach. Tarrant decided to get into administration and White took over in '61. A parent of one of the players on Tarrant's team complained that White wasn't ready to be head coach. White, ever the competitor, got a lot of motivation out of that comment.

He took his first team to a 5-4-1 record. His second team, in '62, finished 3-6. That was White's only losing season as head coach at Banks over 14 years.

He was busy at Auburn in the summers getting his Masters degree in Secondary Education in '61, '62 and '63 and could not make the commitment he wanted for his football team. He was also working a construction job as a clerk for a company at Auburn. Coaches were not paid much at all and he had to have a summer job.

His trips to Alabama, Auburn, Georgia and Tennessee in '63-'64 gave him a game plan for how to run his program. "I learned from Tennessee how to organize practices," he says. "Doug Dickey was their head coach and he was a good guy and a good coach. However, he had a hard time with Alabama."

Meanwhile White had three young children at home and was not there much to be with his kids. He was busy building a career and trying to support his young family. As much as he wanted to be with June and the kids, he had to work. His love for his job kept him at the office late. "I wonder sometimes if my wins and losses would have been any different had I spent more time with June and the kids." He did not neglect his duties as a father though. He cared for and loved his family. June was just such a rock for him taking care of the kids that she allowed him to pursue his profession with a passion. The boys as they grew older came to practices, and Gary played for him. June spent full time raising the children. When the kids started school, she went back to work in education. "She deserves a lot of credit. She helped out later in life earning an income too.

"They weren't problem kids. We would spend the summers at Cascade Plunge (in Birmingham—where White lifeguarded) and stay in the pool. The kids were as content as they could be. I think they looked forward to every day."

White says the '62 team stuck with him because the team just didn't have the talent, though the kids were great and gave maximum effort along with the coaches. They didn't have an experienced quarterback and Woodlawn, Ensley and Ramsay were powerhouses at the time. White had become great friends with his principal, Joe Gann, with whom he went to the Auburn-Nebraska Orange Bowl game—Jimmy had gotten them four tickets for White, Gann and the wives—and "had a ball."

Gann hung in there with White and knew that there just wasn't a lot of talent in '62. The '63 season was a lot better. Led by standouts Bobby Johns and Paige Cutcliffe, David Cutcliffe's older brother, the Jets posted a 6-3 record and beat Woodlawn, their number one rival. "That's when we started building a program," White recalls.

White looks back on Johns's career with admiration. Johns wanted to go to Auburn as a quarterback but Auburn would not offer him a scholarship. White lobbied Alabama to take him. Alabama had Kenny "Snake" Stabler coming to play for them so they were set at quarterback. "I kept telling them they were missing out on a competitor, an athlete," White says.

"Sam Bailey, an Alabama assistant coach, came to a Banks practice and watched Johns, who was playing safety, tackle a running back in a tackling drill. It was a monstrous collision. Pow! Coach Bailey said, 'We'll take him.'"

Johns didn't play his freshman year as freshmen were not allowed to play then. He was an All-Southeastern Conference defensive back his next three years and his junior and senior years he was a consensus All-American. He could have played in the NFL but opted to be a football coach instead, carving out a long career in high school and college football.

Cutcliffe went to Florida and played on teams with Steve Spurrier. "He had a lot of fun too," White says.

White decided that if he wasn't going to outcoach the football coaches in the area, he was going to have to outwork them. There were some stellar coaches in the city and it was a tough go. "I had to work like crazy. I wanted to outwork 'em and outcondition 'em."

White also gained an offensive philosophy from his travels to colleges around the South. He was in Bill Burgess's office when Burgess took over at Woodlawn in the late '60s and saw the University of Houston playbook. White asked Burgess if he could borrow it and Burgess said, "Yeah — it's yours." White took the playbook and studied it intently. White had talked to Erk Russell, the defensive coordinator at Georgia, before he saw the Houston playbook and had seen Houston on film.

One of the Banks's boosters, Marvin Ratcliffe, had a private plane and White told him one summer that he would sure like to go to Houston. Ratcliffe told him he could do it. White spent a couple of days with Coach Willingham at Houston and talked to Bill Yeomen, the head coach. White showed Yeomen the film of his team running the triple option that he had learned from the playbook and Yeomen told him he ran it better than 95 percent of the coaches in Texas, high school or college.

White utilized Gary Rutledge in the triple option and Rutledge ran it to perfection. In '69, Rutledge's senior year, White felt like he had a team that could compete for the state championship at the end of the season, but they had two losses and didn't qualify. White says his '67 team (Johnny Musso's senior year) and his '69 team were teams that could have won the state title. They were playing well enough at the end of the season to do that. Still those teams and his experience in the early '60s along with his state championship in '65, set White up for a terrific run in the early '70s capped by one of the most memorable, probably THE most memorable high school game of all time in Alabama.

*****

Jane Northcutt is Shorty's life-long friend dating back to seventh grade at Graymont Elementary School. She has total admiration and respect for her friend known more for his tough football demeanor than for his vibrant, affable personality, which Northcutt says is a major trait of the coach.

"Shorty was very popular," Northcutt says. "They wanted him to play on the high school team in eighth grade and our teacher, Ms. Allen would take him out there every day for spring practice.

"He was the hardest-working person I've ever known. He took a beating on the football field and he just kept on. I can remember Jimmy Sidle, his brother. Shorty took care of him. Everything that Jimmy knew, Shorty taught him. He loved his brother.

"I never heard Shorty mention his real father. He really had to be the father of his family for many, many years."

Northcutt remembers White as the star running back for the state championship football team at Phillips in 1950.

"He played first string all four years. I just remember his excellence. He was one of the best running backs I ever saw. He had amazing strength. He was a superstar but he was always humble about it. Back when I was in high school people didn't act cocky. I never knew Shorty was a football star. He just had so much humility and honesty. He had that and those are great qualities. He was such a likeable guy. I didn't know anyone who didn't love Shorty White."

Northcutt kept up with her friend through the newspaper while he was at Banks.

"I knew he had a talent to motivate. I read about him every year at Banks and people knew how he raised Jimmy Sidle. He never complained. I imagine he was strict with those boys at Banks but that every one of them knew how much he cared about them."

At the latest reunion of the Phillips High School class of '51, White's good friend and football teammate at Phillips and Auburn, George Rogers, told the group that there would be a book on White.

"He was very humble about it. He always put emphasis on somebody else. Instead of talking about himself, he got up and praised June for running the household on such a small budget when he was coaching. She is lovely. That is real Christianity and that is typical."

Northcutt talked to White at the function and their conversation only enhanced her opinion of him.

"Shorty and I never discussed religion until the other night, but I always knew in my heart that he was a good Christian man. He told me that when the Lord was ready to take him that he was right with the Lord. He said it so humbly. I've known what kind of man he's been for sixty years and he didn't have to say it. He is just that kind of man."

CHAPTER 4
Disappointment on the Plains (1951-1953)

After a highly successful high school football career, White moved on to Auburn to play college football on scholarship and get an education. He also had a football scholarship offer from Ole Miss and to this day believes he could have excelled on the field for the Rebels. But Earl Brown was the coach at Auburn, who Shorty labels a "good guy" who convinced him to come down to the Plains. The Ole Miss coach who recruited White, Johnny Cain, told White that he would start at punter, run back punts and run back kickoffs as a freshman.

Shorty regrets the decision of not going to Ole Miss to this day, but he didn't know that Brown would be fired at Auburn before he started his freshman year and Ralph "Shug" Jordan would become the coach. Jordan was from Georgia and, according to White, "didn't know anything about Alabama football players." Jordan was a big believer in size and White was only 147 pounds so that hurt his chances in Jordan's system.

Still White was always disciplined about practice and worked diligently to be the best player he could be. His schoolwork came along a little bit more slowly. He was not an ambitious student at the time; he failed chemistry in summer school and was taken off scholarship the first quarter of his freshman year. But he got more serious and passed all his courses his first quarter and earned back his scholarship. "My mother had to borrow money to pay my tuition," is how White remembers that first quarter.

During the time that he was not in Graves Center where the football players lived, he would get food from players who would sneak it in from the training table. White says he got in his three squares a day.

He played sparingly his sophomore and junior seasons, but was an eager practice player and always worked on improving his skills. It was something he carried with him later in life as an outstanding football coach. One of his football coaches at Auburn, Gene Lorendo, would have beer waiting for him in his refrigerator at night and told him he could come over to his place after dinner during the week and drink a beer so he could put on some weight. White had to buy a six-pack with his own money for Coach Lorendo. "Every time I went over there, there was only one left," White recalls. "He drank almost every one."

White was the third fastest player on the team his freshman season behind Hoppy Middleton and Jackie Creel. Middleton went on to play for the Detroit Lions.

White did get to carry the ball in the Georgia Tech game his junior year. "I talked my way into the game." He made the most of it, running for 21 yards on his only carry. He never got another carry in the game.

"I never in my wildest dreams thought football was all about size," White thunders. "I thought it was about how much courage you had in your heart." White's frustration with the program grew. It drove him later to excel as a coach.

"I never reached my goals as a player," he says. "That made me hungrier as a coach. You see a lot of Heisman Trophy winners who don't go into coaching because they feel they have achieved all they want to in football. They don't feel like they have anything more to prove. Except for the Ole Ball Coach (Steve Spurrier). Johnny Musso would have been a heckuva coach, but there was no money in it."

But White wasn't through with football. He would later play in the military. "I found out in the military that I was better than they thought I was."

White also boxed. He squared off with an Army Ranger/ Paratrooper from Fort Benning, Georgia on a Saturday. His mother came down to see him that day and had bought him a new watch for his birthday, which was two days away. She didn't like him boxing but let him do what he wanted to do. She always encouraged him to compete. And that he did and did well. That drove him. "She put that drive in me to excel," White remembers. "She was such a good woman."

What White didn't realize then was his mother was about to leave his life tragically.

"It was the last time I saw her," White recalls.

He went on to pummel the Ranger and almost knock him out. The judges gave the fight to the Ranger and the crowd went ballistic in opposition to the decision. There were many Auburn football players down there incensed with the decision. White later found out that all the judges were from Fort Benning. They were all prohibited from judging fights after that.

Two days later, White was called home. His mother had been involved in a car wreck. She and a postman had collided. The man was late going to work and was speeding. To this day White doesn't know whose fault it was. The postman hit Ruth on her side of the car. She fell out the driver's side door and hit her head on the pavement, dying instantly. It was White's 21st birthday. He was told about it while he was at an Auburn basketball game.

"I never heard from him," White says. "I thought he would at least come over and talk to me about it and let me know whether it was his fault, her fault or both their fault. I never got a call, visit or anything. I guess he had his reasons.

"Coach Tarrant and Coach Tucker came by to see me that morning. It made me want to be a coach after they visited me and showed me how much they cared. They didn't say much, they were just there to support me."

The Coach looks back and reflects on his mother and how much of an influence she had on his life and how much he appreciates her to this day for all she gave to him.

"I realize the sacrifices she made in her lifetime," he says. "She had no easy life. She had a tough time on this Earth. I look back and realize that she was a strong person. She provided. I was raised in a one-parent home and I understand today how hard it is. I realize how well I really did have it. It's a shame we don't respect and tell our parents we love 'em until we lose them. I just wish I had one more moment with her to show her my true feelings for her.

"I'm a competitive person and I think I learned that from her. She always stressed not ever giving up and being the best you can be, to do all you can do and that is supposed to be enough. As I grow older I miss her even more. I'll be looking forward to the time I'll meet her again."

A close friend who considers himself like a brother to Shorty, George Rogers was a teammate at Phillips High School and at Auburn; he was a 6-6, 258-pound offensive lineman who was an All-State player in high school. He was considered quite big in his era and Coach Shug Jordan called him and his brother Don, "the two best linemen I ever had at Auburn." The Rogers brothers would "knock the pants off" the defenders, then pick them back up and "dust 'em off." Jordan always said, according to Rogers, "that he couldn't get 'em mean enough."

Rogers played with White for Phillips in the famous Crippled Children's Classic game against Woodlawn at Legion Field that drew a record crowd of 38,000. Phillips won the game and White scored two touchdowns.

Rogers says that White was a diminutive 155-pound running back in high school who would lay the wood to his opponents in practice or in games. He also added what a star he was punting the football.

"He could kick it a ton. He took it as a challenge when a guy tried to tackle him. A lot of guys who tried to tackle him would be lying on the ground. He was tough. There wasn't a back who gave more than Shorty gave. He would throw the halfback pass some. He played both ways and was as tough as anybody on defense. He was All-State his senior year."

White was disappointed at Auburn many times and Rogers believes White's desire to speak his mind got him in trouble.

"When the coach told him he was going to play one week and Shorty told his cousin to come down for the game and he didn't even get in, that disappointed Shorty very much and Shorty told the coaches about it." But honesty in all his matters was an asset also. "It did gain him a lot of success later in life," Rogers says.

Rogers was also on a track relay team with White that tied the state record in the Tuscaloosa Relays.

Rogers says he "admires White" in so many ways but particularly for going back to Jacksonville State and getting his degree after spending time in the military after Auburn.

Rogers remembers vividly White's coaching days. When there were coaches' meetings with the referees—Rogers was a high school referee—White would always be at the meetings drawing up X's and O's. He was totally focused on his profession.

"He would get every advantage he could. There was no doubt in his mind that he could do it. He accomplished so much. He coached a lot of All-Americans and guys who got scholarships to play college football. He made sure his players had their socks and jerseys neatly folded, that there was a neat locker room and shoes were polished. Banks didn't step on the field without looking first-class. It helps you going against your opponent when you look first-class. It's a big advantage for you."

To Rogers, White's experience at Alabama was frustrating because he wasn't as involved in the major coaching decisions as he wanted to be. "He thought he would be more involved. He was real mad at Auburn for the way they treated him as a player."

George does say that White mellowed as he got older.

"At Pleasant Grove (where White finished his career in the early 90's) he realized that there were certain things that he couldn't control and he would not worry about it."

Rogers counts White as a great friend, though he at times was so focused on what he was doing that the friendship at times was not so easy.

"As a friend Shorty was hard to get to know. You had to give a lot more than you took. When Shorty had an opinion he would give it to you whether you liked it or not."

Rogers became a successful businessman selling drugs for a drug company, then running a building business with his brother and finally building metal canopies for gas station pumps. He has endured three bouts with cancer—it has been treated and is in remission; he has also had a heart problem. He has understood the struggle of living a successful and decent life, and through the years he has appreciated the hard work it takes to succeed, and that his friend White put everything he had into his job. Rogers appreciates that, having worked hard himself to support his family and carve out a successful career.

"Nobody in the state deserves to be in the Alabama Sports Hall of Fame more than Shorty. He had a good record as a baseball coach. He would get a book and learn football or baseball. He is a great guy and I admire Shorty very much. He led a life of tough circumstances, losing his dad. He had a good job and today he is just like his old self. He gives you his opinions."

Rogers says that White's opinionated, strong personality was an asset in a lot of instances. He had consistent integrity.

"His word is his bond really. I admire Shorty very much. He is a good friend. He is somebody really special. He would always help other people out. If he could, he would. George Oscar White is a class act in my book."

Rogers notes that White endured a lot of tragedy, losing his mother and his stepdad, whom he was closer to than his own father, who also died when White was young.

"You can't help but feel sorry for Shorty, not that he wants you to. It was tough for him losing his mother. But he accomplished a lot and that is what I'm most proud of him for."

CHAPTER 5
Tragedy Hits, Duty Calls (1953-1955)

White was drafted the fall of his junior year at Auburn by the Army. The summer before he had gone to the Marines' Platoon Leadership Class, a training camp at Quantico, Virginia. It was a rigorous four-week training program that tested mental and physical skills to the max. The mental part was testing different subjects: math, English, geography and science. Its purpose was to see what each trainee's aptitude was.

The physical regimen was intense to say the least. There was hiking up the mountains of Virginia—through fire breaks, places in the mountains where the trees were cut out so fires couldn't spread through the woods—with your pack on your back, your steel helmet, your M-1 rifle on your shoulder and your heavy boots on your feet. The sergeants were just back from Korea and were "mean, tough, bitter guys," according to White.

There was a young, wealthy kid from Buffalo, New York who, White recalls, "had no more business there than a man on the moon." The drill sergeant wanted to work over the young man. The kid had brought his golf clubs, expecting to play some golf on the weekends as there was a course on the base. The sergeant came out to inspect the troops the first day. He looked at the young man and said, "You forgot something, didn't you son?" The boy, according to White, said, "I think I brought everything." The sergeant said, "Go back there and get your @!&# golf clubs."

The sergeant made the young man hike the mountains with his golf clubs and bag strapped to his back. "He fell out a quarter of the way up," White remembers. "They made two guys carry him up the mountain. I was glad I didn't play golf."

The brass decided to make an example of the young man to show that anybody could make it through the program. He tried to quit three or four times but they wouldn't let him. They told him he didn't have to carry the golf clubs up the mountains on the 10-12 mile hikes.

A lot of trainees quit because they couldn't take the physical part. As for White, he was in such tremendous physical shape from his football and boxing that the physical part didn't bother him like it did the others. It was tough but White was fit and had no problem handling it.

White says his training at Quantico was constant.

"The thing that was different is that it was all day," White says, comparing it to football, which was only two to three hours a day. "There were push-ups, sit-ups, side-straddle hops and crawling on your belly for long stretches. It was war preparation, very intense physically and mentally." What impressed White most about the Marines is that the captains who would lead the hikes would give the men a break during the hike and would inspect each man down the line, walking from front to back, and back up to the front. Then the captains would have the men commence walking again. The leaders would never take a break. White says that in the Army the leaders would drive in jeeps inspecting the troops during their hikes.

The guys at Quantico lived for the weekends when they could get away from the constant physical and mental harassment of their sergeants and enjoy some leisure time. White and his buddies would travel: New York City, Washington, D.C., Virginia Beach, Virginia. "We met a couple of gals from Mississippi at the beach," White remembers. "Real class girls. We went sightseeing in New York. We drove Uncle Jim's brand new Olds 88 to Washington. It was great because during the week it was work."

White remembers a grenade drill when he and his fellow troops would get in a ditch and pull clips out of grenades and throw them. "Zoooo, we'd whip those things! They were live grenades so we had to get rid of them."

White recalls an Army exercise even more harrowing than the grenade drill at Quantico: Night Drill. He and the men had to crawl on their bellies under barbed wire with men on the other side shooting over their heads with M-1 rifles. They were shooting straight on and from each side. White said it was a beautiful sight watching it from behind. It looked like radar beams that banks or museums use for their security systems to protect their assets. Shorty was very careful negotiating his crawl.

"If you raised up you were dead. I kept my chin on the ground so I would stay down. That's how I judged if I was low enough."

White remembers one of his friends, a wild man, in a bar once in South Carolina. White was walking up the steps to get to the bar and suddenly two Marines came barreling down the stairs. They had been thrown down the stairs by his friend and another buddy after the Marines had been harassing White's friend about being "a wimp" in the Army. White finished at the top of his class in Army training camp. After the six-week program, he was in the top ten out of the 86 trainees in his class. He earned two stripes and became a corporal. When the training program was ending, the Korean War also came to a close. Had it still been going when White had graduated from the program he would have gone to Korea.

"Nobody wanted to go over there. The odds were not good that you were coming back."

What White heard about Korea is that it was freezing and miserable. There was no warm material in Army clothing so the soldiers froze. He also remembers hearing that it was wet all the time. He heard it was like Alaska. White remembers when he was in high school seeing a lot of West End football players, who were in the Reserves, being called up to report for duty. One of the players, quarterback Bill Burbank, who led West End to the state championship in '49, was involved in an infamous Death March. He survived.

"The guys who went over there, like the guys today who go over to Iraq, are not the same persons when they get home," White says. "They need a lot of help and support from their families and friends."

White remembers General Douglas MacArthur quite fondly. He said that MacArthur built a democracy in Japan—MacArthur was a key leader in World War II. "He went to war to win," White says. "Like most successful people he had an ego. The military would follow him anywhere."

White remembers MacArthur in the Korean War successfully driving the North Koreans back, past the 38th parallel and wanting to drive them farther, past the Yalu Jiang river, farther into China. But President Harry Truman was not of the same mind as MacArthur and fired him for insubordination. White believes that MacArthur would have built a democracy in Korea.

"He loved war," White says of MacArthur. "He would have pushed the Koreans all the way back far into China. In war you need somebody like that. But Washington started running the war. It's like going into the fourth quarter and you're trying to win the ballgame and you put in your second or third string.

"Roosevelt had no use for Truman. Truman did not know about Roosevelt's development of the atomic bomb when it was going on. At least he had guts enough to drop it."

White didn't want to go to Korea because of his little brother

Jimmy who was twelve at the time. White was all Jimmy had for immediate family as both of Jimmy's parents were deceased : White and Jimmy's mother and Lewis, White's stepfather. White was fortunate the war ended before he had to go, but he wasn't through with his training and still wanted to pursue Army training.

"I wasn't afraid, I had a little brother at home who had lost his daddy in World War II and lost his mother in an auto accident. I was the closest kin he had."

He volunteered for jump school at Fort Bragg after the sixteen weeks of training at Fort Jackson, but a week before he was to go, a friend of his, Alex Newton (a lawyer in Birmingham and an officer) called him about where he wanted to go when he finished his training. White told Newton that he had volunteered for Jump School and was heading to Fort Bragg in North Carolina the next week. White believed he would go to Germany with Jump School and didn't want to leave the States and Jimmy, who was living in Birmingham with his Uncle Jim and Aunt Tena, White and Jimmy's mother's brother and his wife.

Newton told White that he had 'volunteered' for jump school and could get out of it and be transferred closer to home. White wanted to go to Fort McClellan in Anniston or Fort Benning in Columbus, Georgia, two places that would allow him to get to Auburn and Birmingham when he could. Newton made that happen and sent the paperwork to the commanding officer at Fort Jackson.

The commander called White in and asked him why he didn't want to go to jump school. White told him that he had one year of eligibility left in football and wanted to eventually get back to school at Auburn. The commander released him and White was commissioned to Fort Benning.

When he was in Army training at Fort Benning, White entered a competition on the base to perform feats of physical fitness at different stations: push-ups, sit-ups, pull-ups on bars and other exercises. White found out after three events that he was in the lead. He was in chief competition with an Army Ranger/Paratrooper. There were four companies competing with about 75 men per company. "I goofed off at the start but after I found out I was in the lead I poured it on." White got to the running events, bore down and won it. He won a three-day pass and a $20 bill.

He would use that station-to-station drill as a coach at Banks. Shorty would have his players work out at different stations five minutes at a time doing different exercises in the off-season before football season. After five minutes, White would blow a whistle and his players would sprint to a different station. He honed his players into top physical condition. This along with fall camp constituted a thorough physical regimen that had his players ready when the season began. No opponent was in better shape than his boys.

"That experience in the military really made me hard-nosed," White remembers. "I saw what preparation was really like. I really and truly believe that most of our wins came from our kids just being tougher. They refused to surrender."

At Fort Benning, White met up with one of his buddies from his high school playing days, Phillip "Rabbit" Smith who had played at Ensley and Alabama. "Rabbit" asked White if he wanted to play football. "I said, 'Heck yeah I want to play football.'" Rabbit got in touch with the coach and White joined the team.

White became a leader immediately. Vince DiLorentes coached the defense and White was captain of the offense and played running back. The captain who originally coached the team left and a new captain took over who didn't know much about football, according to White.

White says that there was a School of Brigade team that considered itself the best team in the Army. They were the officers and they picked players who were big-time college players and players who were in the NFL.

White's team, the 1-3-5 Red Bulls regiment played the School of Brigade and lost by two or three touchdowns. They were competitive, just not as loaded with talent as many other teams.

But they and White saved their best game for the best competition in the military. The Eglin Air Force Base team was a machine. They were undefeated and loaded. The quarterback had played under Coach Bryant at Texas A&M. Boyd Dowler and Max McGee, soon to star with the Green Bay Packers, were the wide receivers. Dowler and McGee were key players on the Packers' Super Bowl Championship teams of 1967 and 1968.

When White and his teammates were warming up, the Eglin team hit the field for their pre-game warm-ups. White says it was like looking at the Washington Redskins with their maroon stripes and white pants. "We were a bunch of misfits going against a machine. It was Thanksgiving Day. They were dressed so nice and they were big-name players."

White says in the dressing room the team was scared. The captain said that they could put their uniforms up and go back to Fort Benning. Joe Dinay, one of White's teammates, started laughing and said, "Let's go out there and see what happens."

On the opening drive, Eglin drove it down the field and scored. The Red Bulls then got a first down but punted. White punted. Eglin drove down the field again and scored to go up 13-0. But the Red Bulls blocked the extra point. "The game was on radio throughout the state of Florida," White recalls. After the blocked extra point, White grins, "the tide turned." White's team started moving the ball and scored to make it 13-7 at halftime.

In the second half the Red Bulls outscored Eglin 25-0 and won the game 32-13. "That was the best game I ever played in my life," White says. "We couldn't do anything wrong."

White had scored on a 20-plus yard run and a 30-plus yard run. He had big rushing gains throughout the game. "That game did so much for my confidence. I knew right then that I could play with the big boys."

White says that after the game he and a friend were trying to go to the Alabama-Auburn game. He was about to leave when the chef emerged from the kitchen. "He was looking for little number eleven," White says. He fixed a box of food and "I was fed like I've never been fed before."

White has some great stories from his days playing football at Fort Benning. Once White was back in punting formation during a game and he saw that Billy Tease, an All-American cornerback, was running back to cover the kick and that all the opposing team was rushing inside. When White got the snap he took off running. "It was wide open on the right side," White says. "Billy Tease was running back to block and I followed him all the way down the field."

White remembers the hardest hit he ever received was from Frank Kush, later head coach at Arizona State and the Baltimore Colts. "He was about 185 pounds. He was blocking for the kickoff return team. I was either the outside guy on kick coverage or the first man inside of him. When I went down there he knocked me into the spikes of the other players. I lost my breath and then I threw up. He played at Michigan State. There were athletes all over the bases."

Joe Dinay was on White's team. Dinay would take care of the laundry for many of the men or rather he'd take it home to his wife and charge each man 50 cents per bag. Dinay would call the bags, "fluff bags." Dinay would say, "Give me your fluff!", White remembers. "Dinay would bring it back on Mondays folded up. "He'd look like Santa Claus with all those bags of fluff."

For White, Fort Benning wasn't bad at all especially since he was playing football. He still had to get up at 6 a.m. for roll call and breakfast but there was free time since the football players had free time. White didn't have to do field work because of football.

White had played baseball in the military. He talked the coach into letting him play for the team and told him he could get the team a game with Auburn. White pitched an inning in one game. He had never been taught to rotate his hips when he was pitching so he was all arms when he threw the ball. He hit the first batter he faced. The batter looked at him sternly. "He was a big guy. I thought he was coming out to get me." Shorty walked the next guy and hit the next, but the following batter hit a hard grounder to the shortstop who threw to third for an out and then the third baseman threw home for a double play. The next batter hit one deep to center field but the center fielder made the catch and White got out of the inning unscathed. His arm was dragging when he left the mound. "I never wanted to do that again. Plus we got our tails whipped."

White was about to be discharged from the Army in 1955 after months in the military when he found out his father had been killed in a fire in a warehouse in Birmingham. He was smoking and had fallen asleep. He perished in the fire caused by the cigarette. "He had never been around. I thought back to if he and my mother had gotten along and he could have been my dad. The funeral was in the west side of town and I was let out to go to the funeral. Then I came back and was discharged. I was a free man."

White remembers driving out of the base and waving to the guards at the gate and not stopping. "It was a great experience."

After the service, the football coach of Jacksonville State, Don Salls, told White he could come to Jacksonville and have two more years of eligibility. He was on scholarship and he also had the GI Bill, which would pay for school. Auburn was only going to give him one more year and White believed he would not get a shot at playing, given the size of the players that Auburn was recruiting. White chose Jax State and started the next phase of his life that involved football and an enduring romance.

CHAPTER 6
Graduation, June, Sylacauga (1955-1959)

White returned from the Army and earned a two-year scholarship to play and attend school at Jacksonville State. He liked the deal at Jax State because he could get two years and receive money from the GI Bill, extra money that he needed. He wanted to play football for two more years and Jax State offered him that opportunity. White regrets that Auburn would not give him much chance at playing time because of his size. He to this day doesn't understand that philosophy.

He played most games at Jax State. Shorty punted and returned punts and played in the offensive backfield. "We had some good teams," he remembers. "One year we lost just one game. We wanted to play Alabama but they wouldn't play us. We'd probably have beaten them."

White was on a team that went to the Refrigerator Bowl in Evansville, Indiana against Rhode Island. "We knocked their quarterback out in the first quarter. We beat the stew out of 'em. I've still got the silver bowl from the game." Jax State played and beat teams like Chattanooga and Troy State in Division 1-AA ball.

White also got a great education. At Auburn he was in survey classes with 150 other students in an auditorium. At Jax State there was more individual attention in classes. He liked the professors and had a counselor who took a keen interest in his progress. White became a good student at Jacksonville and earned a B average.

His counselor found out that White wanted to get into coaching and lined him up with the superintendent of Sylacauga schools, Dr. Martin, and the principal at Sylacauga High School, Dr. Poarch. White had offers to be the head football coach at Southside Gadsden and become the assistant football coach at Heflin with the promise of being the head football coach in his second year. "I knew I wasn't ready to be a head football coach in high school," he admits. So White took the job at

Sylacauga as the seventh, eighth and ninth grade coach.

Before that, during his junior year at Jax State, White had met a young woman from Birmingham-Southern College, June Melton. His cousin, Robert Thornton, who was in school at Birmingham-Southern, told White about June. "He told me, 'I'm going to introduce you to the girl you're going to marry.' I told him, no way!"

On their first date White and June went to a movie. White was afraid she might be too tall for him. "I didn't want to marry anyone taller than me." White is 5-foot-8.

White and June kept going out on dates and he liked her more and more. "We double-dated a lot," he says. "We went out with her friends and double-dated with Bobby Duke (White's teammate at Phillips who was the quarterback). June had told White that she wasn't going to marry anyone without a college degree. White knew he needed to get one. He was also very ambitious to be a teacher/coach and he told June that he didn't know how much money was in it. She said that was fine with her. "She has been instrumental not only in our marriage, but in my entire life," White says. "She got me on the straight and narrow. June has been the biggest plus of my life. She has always encouraged me and she's done very little complaining. I don't know how she put up with me really. She has a very strong constitution. She has calmed me down and my manners have improved."

White says that June was always there when he needed her after games, particularly after losses that occurred early in his career at Banks before White had his program established and winning regularly.

"It was quiet at home after losses but she always said, 'you can't win 'em all. You've got another one next week. You can do it next week!'" The Whites were married August 25, 1956 just before his senior season. They went to Gulf Shores for their honeymoon for a week. "It was nice, quiet and peaceful. We had the whole beach to ourselves."

White finished up his senior year, then after offers came in, he decided to go to Sylacauga. Once he accepted the job at Sylacauga, White told the Sylacauga leaders that he wanted to split the football team between the seventh and eighth graders as one team and the ninth grade along with the tenth graders who didn't make the varsity as the other team. He would call the ninth and tenth grade team his B team and the seventh and eighth graders his middle school team. The principal, Dr. Poarch allowed him to do that.

White was now coaching two teams. "It was a lot of work, you bet," he says.

Ed Dark was a volunteer coach, his only other coach, to help him out. Dark's dad owned Dark Dairy. "I got a lot of free milk. I needed that with young kids in the house."

White would have the seventh and eighth graders the last period of school from 2-3 p.m. so he could work with them before the ninth and tenth graders came out to practice. He would teach technique and line assignments and also work with the backs and receivers while Dark would put them through running drills.

"I would teach my linemen to block inside, block outside and if they weren't there, block the linebacker. They were simple rules."

The rules he taught worked and worked quickly. White's first year went well but the second year both teams went undefeated. "We played Pell City and beat them 56-0 the first time we played 'em. We were supposed to play 'em again but they cancelled the game."

One player who White remembers vividly was a huge lineman whom White took an interest in. He couldn't run; White took some weight off him so he could. White put the young boy at nose guard. White aligned him over the center and coached him to run through a gap. "He couldn't tackle but he could eliminate folks."

His dad ran a big fruit stand called Yonder's Blossom. "I couldn't remember his name, so I called him Yonder's Blossom. He had a ball playing."

White tried to talk to the head varsity coach, Tom Calvin, to stick with Yonder's, but he didn't. "That was a waste." White remembers a varsity football player smarting off to him before a practice. He was calling to White, "Hey, Shorty!"

"I was a youthful-looking guy." White went over to Coach Calvin: "I am fixing to whip one of your players. He didn't call me coach, he called me Shorty. Coach Calvin said 'ok'."

White took the boy to a room and told that "big sucker" that he would address him as "Coach" or "Coach White" and was going to show him respect. And if he didn't, "We were going to have another meeting like we're fixing to have."

White paddled the kid. "I gave him a couple of whoopees, which were soon followed by 'I get the message coach.'" After that White had no problems with that kid or any other kid on the team. White's message rang out loud and clear. He was not to be disrespected.

White told Dr. Martin and Dr. Poarch at his interview that he wanted to start a track team at Sylacauga. He was already teaching four classes: three history classes and a PE class. "I wanted to be a head coach. It was important for my future. They said, 'I don't see why not.'"

White took a busload of kids down to Montgomery for the state indoor track meet in the winter of his first year at Sylacauga. "The kids fell in love with it," he says. So White bought a couple of hurdles, a shot put, some batons and shorts and t-shirts. He got the kids to buy their track shoes. He got a good deal for them buying in bulk.

Coach Calvin was against White's idea of a track team because he didn't want White to take away any of his baseball players. (Calvin was the varsity baseball coach.) He confronted White, who said that there were some football players out there who didn't play baseball and that they needed a sport to play to keep them active in sports. Plus track was great physical training for football.

"I told Calvin that track would build endurance, speed and quickness and that it would be a credit to the football program."

Calvin thought White's explanation was reasonable and agreed with him that track was indeed good for the athletic program.

White took the reins of the track program and it took off, as all of White's coaching ventures did. The first year White's team won the district and finished second at the sectional meet. The second year, Sylacauga won the district, the sectional and finished second or third in the state.

White took all the trophies up to Dr. Martin's office and said that the program needed a track. Dr. Martin agreed and built a track around the football field. The next year when White moved on to Banks, the school won the state. They also won it the following year.

"I love track and field—it is second to football for me," White says. "I had decent speed when I was in grammar school but I wasn't really that fast. It really helped me."

The experience at Sylacauga was rewarding:

"It was a great experience. Jimmy and I were pulling a trailer down from Jacksonville to go to Sylacauga, and June and I had just had Gary. The trailer fell off the truck; we had stuff everywhere. When I started at Sylacauga I couldn't spell it.

White spent two high-quality years at Sylacauga, then he had an offer to start a new position at Banks High School. He took the offer. It was a decision that led to one of the most successful and lasting legacies in Alabama high school sports.

CHAPTER 7
Back with Tarrant (1959-1961)

Coach Tarrant moved from Phillips to Banks where White was his assistant football coach, B team basketball coach and B team track coach in his first two years on the job from 1959-61. His football acumen helped the varsity team under Coach Tarrant, a very fine football coach in his own right, win the city championship in 1960. The team went 5-4-1 and White helped lay the foundation for a program that would become a dynasty in the early 70's. The Jets won the Clinic game played at Legion Field before 30,000 people, 28-0 over Ensley. White would not know this at the time, but he would soon become the leader at Banks and assume responsibility for the football program, a job he would cherish and excel at.

He established himself as a versatile coach in all sports. As B team basketball coach in the early years, White resorted to his hard-nosed style of driving his players to be the best they could be. His B team was not performing up to expectations. In White's eyes they weren't tough enough. So he brought out the boxing gloves one day and had his players box each other. "I was going to toughen 'em up," he chuckles. "We had played Woodlawn the game before and they had thrown cherry bombs at my players' feet and they got intimidated."

Word had spread about White having his players box the day before, so parents were out in full force the next day at practice. White knew this when he went out on the court, but he was not going to change his approach. That's the Shorty White way. White gave his players an option that they were either going to box again or play winning basketball. The players chose the latter. For the next 45 minutes, White conducted three-on-three rebounding drills on the free throw line. The team never lost again the rest of the season. "I was pleased, I was satisfied. They received the message." White's team lost their opening game against Talladega after not having practiced one time because of football and they lost the Woodlawn game but didn't lose another. White had established himself as a guy who could win in any sport.

White and Dewell Crumpton, "the best track coach I've ever been around," handled the varsity track team. White was coach of the B team and the assistant to Crumpton on the varsity. White and Crumpton led their teams to many state runs with Banks competing for titles, though not attaining one. Murphy of Mobile was dominant at the time, but Crumpton and White's teams were highly competitive, always in the championship mix. White and Crumpton took their team down to Prichard for a meet at Vigor High School with teams from the Mobile area and a team from Florida featuring one of the fastest high hurdlers White had ever seen. White realized that his B team could do as well as his varsity runners. White called Tarrant at 10:30 the night before the meet and said that the B team needed to be in Mobile. Tarrant was furious at White for calling him so late, but he and four of the B teamers did make it to Mobile, leaving Birmingham at 2:30 a.m., arriving around 7 a.m. White says that Tarrant hit a cow or a horse on the way down as he was driving as quickly as possible. "He was a sport!"

Tarrant made it down that morning for the race. The team finished second. Jimmy Sidle and the kid from Florida had one of the best races White has ever seen with the kid from Florida nicking Sidle at the wire. Both were state champions. Sidle was never beaten in Alabama.

Albert Morton coached the basketball team and with standouts like Sidle, a tremendous all-around athlete, and George Morris, made it all the way to the state championship game where they lost to Tuscaloosa 57-55.

Crumpton and White took their athletes in track and got them to compete beyond their ability.

White was now teaching three history classes and two PE classes at Banks. Tarrant decided to become a principal so the head football coaching job was up for grabs in 1961. White, of course, wanted it. He was 30 years old. Coach Tarrant and the principal wanted Earl Gartman to become the coach. Gartman was not coaching at the time. The Board wanted Jim Pyburn who played at Ensley and Auburn and was the assistant coach at Woodlawn.

Mack Shoemaker, a sportswriter for *The Birmingham News*, was pushing White for the job.

"I asked him, "What are you trying to do?" White remembers. "And he said he was on my side. He helped me get the job."

Tarrant and Mr. Gann, the principal, did not want Pyburn and the

Board wouldn't consider Gartman. So White got the job by the process of elimination.

"From the first day I coached I wanted to be a head coach," White says. "I didn't like being an assistant at Banks, Sylacauga and at Alabama (from 1975-81). I wanted to be in charge. That's the ego in all coaches. I wanted to do things my way."

White says that coaching at Banks in the early years was like "running in the Kentucky Derby with a donkey. The physical talent was not there."

White was also spending his first few summers at Auburn getting his Masters degree in Secondary Education. He lived at Auburn in the summers and worked a construction job doing clerical work keeping up the payroll, scheduling the work and other duties. White, who had worked many physically demanding jobs earlier in life, couldn't afford to have a physically intense job because he was in school and needed to spend much of his time on his schoolwork. He used the money from his work to pay for his education.

White would get to the library in the morning, attend classes all day and spend time in the library at night. There wasn't much time for anything else except spending time with June and Gary during his down time, which was minimal as he was working too.

Looking back, he couldn't spend the quality time with the football team that he wanted to those first three summers.

"We made up for it when I got through with school," he says. "We rolled up our sleeves and got to work."

White got his Masters from Auburn. His plan was to bring in more income for his family and the advanced degree would allow him to do that. He was as serious about education as he was about football.

When White was an assistant under coach Tarrant at Banks, he saw Jimmy as an athlete who had great God-given talent but was not big on practice. "Coach Tarrant did an excellent job of preparing Jimmy," White says.

"He didn't like to practice, but he was a competitor," White declares. "He didn't like lifting weights. He was strong from the waist down." White believes Sidle got hurt at Auburn because he didn't lift weights. "He would play three-on-three basketball all day. He would also play hurt. His elbow was bulging and he got antibiotics and wrapped the elbow up before a game and played. He played like there was nothing wrong with him."

Sidle had that toughness like his brother to go along with superior athletic skills. Jimmy went on to Auburn and was an All-American his junior year as a quarterback. During Sidle's junior year he got hurt in the Alabama game and Mailon Kent took over at quarterback. When asked if he was ready to come back in from his injury, Sidle said, "This is Kent's game to win." Kent led his team to victory.

When Sidle was being recruited by colleges for football, Furman Bisher, the famous columnist and reporter for *The Atlanta Journal-Constitution*, came over to Birmingham to interview White and June. "He wanted to see if we were getting something under the table from Auburn," White thinks. Times were tough. For example, there was no furniture in the living room. Bisher was so impressed with White and June that he wrote a highly complimentary article on White, June and Sidle. White had only asked Auburn to do one thing for him. Get Sidle a job in the summer so he could stay busy, make some money and stay out of trouble. Auburn complied. White always looked after his brother and gave him all the support and love he had to give. White was the father figure that Sidle needed.

White was committed to teaching history along with his PE classes and coaching duties at Banks. "You had to be," he maintains. "There was no other option. Banks was trying to get accredited as a high school at the time and there were people coming in who would sit in your classroom, observe you and take notes."

White was critiqued regularly by the school as well, and he was very serious about his teaching responsibilities. He loved history.

White would tell his students to learn as much about history as they possibly could because history repeats itself and one learns from the past how to handle the future.

White particularly liked the study of World War II and American generals of that era. He admired George Patton and Douglas MacArthur the most. He was a strong field general himself in athletics and had military training that he conveyed to his athletes; he appreciated what strong leaders had accomplished in their careers on the battlefield. He says today that with Patton, MacArthur, Norman Schwarzkopf and Colin Powell, the U.S. would not be in the situation it is in Iraq. These leaders would have taken care of the insurgents and won the war in the Middle East.

White's classroom was serious. He had good kids who wanted to get a good education. When they got out of line and disrupted class, White would send them to the hall and tell them they had a couple of options: either go to the principal and lose class time and have their grades lowered every day, or, act properly. He also would use the academic paddle. When his players made a C in class they would get one lick, a D would earn them two and an F, three.

White recalls that when he was a student at Phillips, Coach Tucker and Coach Tarrant used the paddle on him. "When I coached with Coach Tarrant he gave me a lick. It worked."

For White, "Everything was above board in school. If you did a good job in the classroom and you didn't abuse the kids you'd keep your job even if you didn't win a game." Academics came first, though White never had a problem winning games.

White's first four years as head football coach were on-the-job training. He was young, trying to get his Masters at Auburn during the summers of '61, '62 and '63 and he didn't have a particular offensive or defensive philosophy. His '61 team went 4-4-1, his '62 team was 3-6 (his only losing season in 14 years at Banks), his '63 team finished 6-3 and his '64 team posted a 5-4 mark. That approach changed before the '65 season. And his fortunes were really going to change as he was about to establish an enduring legacy of excellence in high school football at Banks High School.

But Shorty didn't do it alone. For example, consider the record of Dewell Crumpton, one of White's oldest friends and closest confidants. Crumpton, a terrific athlete and a tremendous track coach at Ramsay and at Banks, has the utmost respect for his best friend whom he calls one of the best coaches he's ever been associated with.

Crumpton set three state records as a high hurdler, low hurdler and high jumper at Ramsay High School in the 50's. He also played defensive end on the football team. Dewell received a track scholarship to Alabama and set the Southeastern Conference record for high hurdles in indoor track. He went to Phillips to coach after college and served under Coach Tarrant, with White.

Dewell got to know White and said he was full of energy and "very intense. He loved coaching and he loved coaching football."

Crumpton knows White was obsessed with coaching. "When people are really good at something they are obsessed with it."

Dewell reflects on White's tunnel vision when it came to coaching: "He was totally determined to be a coach and nothing was going to stop him. That is what attracted me to him. He was totally dedicated to what he was doing."

Crumpton observed how White would settle for nothing less than the best out of his athletes. When Tarrant retired, Crumpton knew how badly White wanted the job. "He wanted that job with all his heart."

When White took over the first year and the team went 4-4-1, White was the first guy there in the morning and the last to leave. He was all about cleanliness in the locker room and he was determined to instill pride in the program.

"It never dawned on the man he was going to be a loser," Crumpton says. "He kept on giving everything he had."

Crumpton went into the service with the Army Airborne in '63 and that is when White started winning at Banks. "He was the head man, no question about it," Crumpton notes. "He had a plan and he put it in place and believed in himself. He took his falls and accepted his responsibilities. He was his own man. I admire him for that."

Crumpton calls White "unique" because in high school he won a state championship as a player, then he won three as a coach at Banks and then, as an assistant at Alabama, won two national championships in '78 and '79. "He knew how to instill a winning attitude in his kids. He was way ahead of his time in weight training. No one lifted weights in high school then. Some parents were against it, but he stayed true to his wishes."

After serving active duty with the Army Rangers, Crumpton came back to coach with Mutt Reynolds at Ramsay. Banks played Ramsay and Ramsay kept it very close, losing 7-0. White and Banks thought they might win handily. Crumpton says that was a tribute to Reynolds, an excellent football coach in his own right. There was mutual respect between the two coaches. "Those were two teams that were totally prepared. I loved that game. They had respect for each other."

Crumpton became head coach at Huffman in the late 60's while White was becoming a legend. "Wherever he's been he's won and he hasn't just won, he's won big. In doing all that, he's had tremendous character. He was able to instill desire and character in his kids. He cared about them. He cared a whole lot more than just winning. There is a soft side to him that I recognize."

Crumpton says that what is even more impressive about White is that he accomplished so much and cared about other people so much, particularly his kids, despite the fact that he had to overcome tremendous hardship in life.

"If you want to look around for excuses, he had 'em all. He was poor and came from a rough side of town. But he refused to fail and became, I think, one of the great coaching leaders in Alabama."

In track, Crumpton, a master at it, says that White, despite his love for football, was committed to the sport. "We had no ulterior motives. I was for the kids and he was for the kids. He took the B team track team very seriously. Whatever he coached, he put everything he had into it."

White and Crumpton are best of friends today. "He calls me once a week. He is a really true friend. Nobody worked harder than him. He worked for what he believed in. He's a phenomenal person."

Another great help to Shorty, particularly in the early years at Banks, was Albert Morton, a highly successful basketball coach at Banks from '57-'64, who took his Banks teams to 20-plus win seasons. One of his teams went to the state championship game, finishing the season 30-4 before losing to Tuscaloosa in the state title game. Banks won the city and county championships that year.

Morton also coached B team football and coached kids on the '63 team who went on to win the state championship in '65. He went into administration after his Banks tenure and became principal at Huffman, where he served for 28 years.

He remembers White as "very, very dedicated and intense," a man who took a boy on the B team, Mike Luther and toughened him up with some physical practices that included boxing matches with other players. Luther became a standout at Banks, an All-State player. He became the all-time leading scorer at Birmingham-Southern and has been chosen for the BSC Hall of Fame. He now works for NASA.

Morton also had teams finish 25-6 and 19-7. He had solid teams fundamentally that played with tenacity and were highly skilled. He was a master at basketball.

He went on to become a state legislator for District 45 representing eastern Birmingham, the Irondale, Leeds and St. Clair County areas. "I enjoyed it. I also sold residential real estate for Martin Demedicis Realty." Morton now lives in Cropwell on Lake Logan Martin. Morton remembers White's decision to pull out the boxing gloves after a game against Woodlawn. "It was the first area game and we weren't aggressive. We weren't going after the loose balls. It embarrassed Coach. He was not going to have the boys play like that. So he got the boxing gloves out and said, 'Who wants to play?' He wanted his kids to get after the other team."

"Mike Luther was a big clumsy kid but he had a lot of heart and character. He became All-City and All-State. Coach White and I brought that out of him.

"There was no fooling around with Coach White. He had that Nick Saban attitude. He loved football. After the kids boxed in practice, the mommas wanted to run him off, but he fended them off."

Morton talks about some of the players who played football and basketball at Banks under him and White. George Morris went to Georgia Tech to play football, and Larry Camp also went there. Bobby Johns was an All-American twice in football at Alabama; he played for

White and Morton. And Jimmy Sidle was an outstanding basketball player for Morton.

"Coach White should be in the Alabama Sports Hall of Fame," Morton insists. "He has a good record and developed highly successful young men. He worked hard at it."

Take a look at the record: White was 100-37-3, a 71% winning percentage playing against the top competition in the state in Birmingham, powerhouses Woodlawn, Ensley, West End and Ramsay among others. It was a highly competitive time in high school football and White's teams were dominant for most of his 14 years at Banks, as his three state championships show.

CHAPTER 8
Learning the Ropes (1961-1964)

In his first two years at the helm at Banks, White was busy in the summers getting his Masters degree in Secondary Education at Auburn. It was tough for him to focus on football because he was busy with his schoolwork. He was handicapped due to his academic responsibilities and would only get back to Birmingham just in time for summer practice. They were lean years record-wise because the team was just getting its legs underneath it and there wasn't a stable of talent at Banks.

White did conduct spring drills before the '61 season and when he came back for fall drills in August he wanted to test his players' conditioning to see if they had worked out and stayed in shape over the summer. There were many "gassers" and mile runs in the summer. White always had that disciplined approach to the game and he instilled it from the beginning of his tenure. No weight room at Banks? No problem— White would soon change that in the next couple of years.

White's best player, Greg Henry, a 6-1 transfer from Woodlawn came down with mononucleosis before the '61 season and was lost for the year. "We just didn't have the talent to win big," Shorty notes.

But White did intend to instill discipline in his players and he wanted to teach character and class, not just X's and O's. "I wanted to try and make 'em think competitively and bring out discipline in them. I did not have a lot of X's and O's. But we were going to work harder than anybody we played. We were going to be conservative in everything we did. I was learning."

White did have his critics. A parent of a player on the '60 team told White that he didn't think he was ready to be head coach. White, true to his competitive nature, became more driven because of that comment. He counted on his competitive drive and what he learned from his predecessor, Coach Tarrant, his Auburn and Jacksonville State playing experience and his years in the military.

"I had an old Auburn playbook," he says. "We ran basic hand-off plays and tried to throw the ball a little bit. We also ran a screen. We scored on a screen against Robert E. Lee in a 7-7 tie. They went on to go undefeated."

White says he didn't have time to study the game his first two years. He gained knowledge from other people like Bear Bryant. He learned about defense and organization from Tennessee. He would later learn a Russian weight-training regimen from Georgia that he effectively employed at Banks, which led to some spectacular years beginning in 1965. It was a maximum and minimum weightlifting program: a player would keep working up on the pounds on the bar, lifting as many repetitions as possible, and then maxing out and going back down on the pounds. It made his players a lot stronger and increased their endurance on the field.

White did gain a lot of confidence in himself when his team tied R. E. Lee in the first game of the '61 season, 7-7. Lee was the three-time defending state champion.

"The student body and the principal gained more confidence in me," White says. I knew I was mentally and physically strong. I just had to instill that in my football players."

White went 4-4-1 in 1961. His '62 team was his worst record-wise. They were 3-6. "I was really handicapped in the summers when I was in school," he says. "There was no way I could give those kids what they deserved."

White didn't have the luxury of summer football camps like they have today. He didn't have a weight room, but he built one in '63 with the help of his students, parents, a contractor, a plumber and bricklayers. White built it from the ground up; it paid huge dividends in the following years and led to a state title in '65 and highly successful seasons after that.

White had kids at home. He says there wasn't much time for family life because he was almost overwhelmed with his responsibilities. He was teaching five academic classes, head coaching football, coaching B team basketball and helping out coaching track. In the summers he was a lifeguard at Cascade Plunge in Birmingham. Teachers/coaches were not paid in the summer; White had to make a living so there was no vacation. Vacations were limited to the swimming pool at Cascade Plunge.

White and June and the children moved to 85th street; his backyard ran down to the high school. The house had four bedrooms, two bathrooms, a living room, an eating area and a basement. Two of his players, Bobby Johns and Paige Cutcliffe helped move White and to them the house didn't look very big from the outside. They helped paint it and did some work on it. "They said, 'Coach we didn't think you improved any.'"

White had to do his share of disciplining players his first two years. He kicked off a player who broke rules. There was some smoking on the team and some drinking.

"I was too stern the first couple of years," he recalls. "There is nothing gained from kicking a player off the team. But a coach doesn't want to lose the rest of the players if he doesn't discipline one. You might lose 'em all. It's a necessity."

White was blessed with players, for the most part, willing to make the commitment to his plan. "We had a good work ethic. They were good kids. They did exactly what you told 'em to do and then some."

White learned a lot about X's and O's his first two years. And he always stressed the kicking game. He says to this day that it is just as important as defense and offense. He really stresses defense and the kicking game because if the other team doesn't score, they can't beat you. His offense took off years later as he employed a lot of play-action passes and a superior running game, which led to state championships.

"We worked on punting, punt coverage, punt returning, kickoff coverage and kickoff return. Offense was the last thing we worked on. You put all three phases together and you've got a state title contender."

Another part of his job was dealing with the media and White was good at that. Ronald Weathers and Herbie Kirby were the mainstays of *The Birmingham News's* high school coverage in the early '60s. Alf Van Hoose mainly wrote about colleges but wrote a great piece on the Clinic game one year, according to White.

"They weren't like some of the guys today looking for something negative to write," White says. "A guy for *The News* wrote that I should get the job at Banks and helped me get it. They were positive."

"If I said something that didn't come out right and might hurt somebody else's feelings, they would ask me if I really wanted to say that. They would talk me out of it. Ron Ingram of *The News* today is a pretty positive guy also. Today a lot of the guys are just waiting for you to say something wrong."

While the sportswriters today have plenty to write about that is negative—and much of what they write about is the truth—White liked the way writers handled things in the old days. There are still plenty of positive things to write about today and plenty of positive articles in *The*

News. White listens to some sports radio shows also.

"Some of them are pretty good," he says. "Some are not interesting."

White is not so diplomatic on the subject of rules and regulations for winning football teams. Shorty was a true believer in setting rules and following them when it came to leading his teams. I said it seemed that all of his players were scared of him. "I would like to think they respected me," he responded.

It was both. White simply says that in his program, "The rules put before them were meant to be followed."

He kicked off a player in 1961, his first year, who was an SEC-caliber player. White says if a player was not going to follow the rules he would not be part of his football team. "I don't know how you run a football program if you don't have discipline."

White is distraught over the way college athletes break all kinds of rules. He says he picks up the paper every day and sees another kid in college getting a DUI or a public drunkenness charge or an assault charge and it disgusts him. "It didn't happen back then and when it did those infractions were few and far between."

There is no doubt that college players drank, back in the 30's through the 60's, but it didn't seem to be as rampant and there was more respect for authority. "It ruins the sports not only if you're trying to win but when you're trying to build character. You've got to sell 'em on morals. It pays off for you positively."

White attributes his disciplined regimen for his players to his military training. He says his ex-players who served in the military later "verified what I was trying to develop in the players. It was in their best interest."

White ran a tight ship exhorting his players to keep clean lockers, be at practice on time, never to loaf. He expected that of himself. If the players broke the rules they would run or get paddled; there was no grey area with his discipline. He expected his players to never argue with a referee's call. He believes that was his job.

White had a big day coaching against R.E. Lee in his first year. The Jets, who according to White lacked material in 1961, tied Lee 7-7. It was a Lee team that finished the season 8-0-1 and captured the state championship as voted on by the sportswriters. (State playoffs weren't instituted until 1966.)

"They were well coached and had better talent than we did," White recalls. "I don't know how we did it."

White had been in Auburn during the summers of '61, '62 and '63 and couldn't spend any time with his players. "I was really handicapped then," he says. But in '64 he was back in charge in the summer and had many conditioning drills and started getting his players "on the steel."

His weightlifting program started paying huge dividends and paid off fully with a state championship in 1965.

Ramsay under legendary coach Mutt Reynolds had beaten Banks from '61-'64. Reynolds was another disciplinarian whom White looked up to.

But White got over the hump in '65, beating Ramsay twice during the Jets' undefeated season, once during the regular season, and then in the Clinic game, showcasing the best two teams in the city at the end of the season.

White's '66 team finished 7-2. They lost to Ramsay 10-0 and Jones Valley 14-6.

"There were great coaches in the area and great coaches in the state." White mentions Reynolds, Tom Jones of Lee in Montgomery and Johnny Howell of Woodlawn. It was a highly competitive time for football in the city and throughout the state.

White's '63 team featured two players who went on to play college football : Bobby Johns—who later coached for White at Banks before moving up to college coaching—after starring at Alabama for three years at defensive back; and Paige Cutcliffe, who went on to play at Florida. "The rest of the kids gave great effort but they lacked speed and size." The '63 team went 6-3.

"Nobody expected a lot from us," Johns remembers. "We had Sam Chambliss who would have been an SEC player had he kept up his grades. Coach took care of us and got us great equipment. He made it a big deal to play for the Jets."

"He was such a focused guy. Whatever he was doing, he was a competitor."

Johns confirmed White's opinion that the paddle was very effective. "Coaches were allowed to do that then. He would bring us in on the bleachers when grades came out and if anybody had an F, he would paddle their backside. If anybody wanted to be eligible they would take their whipping and get to work on school."

Johns also says that he gained great coaching experience under White. "He was so into what he was doing. He loved it. We were rebuilding a couple of years that I was there. He would do anything to get an edge on his opponent. He was a good one. I couldn't have had a better teacher."

Johns went on to coach at North Alabama, then called Florence State, and was the head coach at West Alabama and back in the high school ranks at Pleasant Grove and McAdory.

"He was about doing the right things. There was not one player who wasn't expendable if he didn't follow the rules. He made sure there was no doubt who the boss was."

"In the summers when I was coaching, we would spend a lot of the time getting the field ready. He would teach us to shine our shoes and have the locker room cleaned up. I am a neat freak about folding clothes today because of him."

Johns says that the players from White's teams don't understand why he is not in the Alabama Sports Hall of Fame.

"I never can understand that. It's a shame he is not in the Hall." Johns is impressed that White keeps up with his players today and has been "a great father figure" to many of his former players.

"He's always been there. He's as steady as a rock."

From '61-'63, White couldn't be at Banks in the summer. "It was killing me. I couldn't ask my assistant coaches to do it because they were getting 12 months pay over nine months and they weren't paid much money at all. They had to get jobs. It was tough."

White is convinced that he got his strength to carry on with his profession from June, his wife. "She never complained. When I told her we didn't have money to pay the bills she would get us to go to the credit union and borrow money. Wives of coaches were tougher than we were."

While he was the ultimate disciplinarian and warrior, White says his players had it much better under him than under some of the coaches of the past. "Kids didn't know how good they had it then even under me," muses Shorty.

White had two team doctors who performed surgery on his players. One of his surgeons, James Faulkner was "ahead of his time" on knee surgery. His players would go to Faulkner and White says almost to a man, the players would come back ready to play. "He was outstanding."

White would work with his players on exploding off the ball, using their hips to lead the way. Jack Dempsey, the famed boxer of the 20's and 30's, was his model for exploding with the hips. "He could stand six inches from the side of a cow and knock it on its side with a punch, Boom!"

White would use that six-inches theory in his paddling of players who made an F in school. He would line that paddle up close and smack his players on their rear ends. "The paddle would do some talking."

To White, a boxer going three two-minute rounds was like playing two football games in a row. It was exhausting. Boxers would rotate their hips to throw a punch and that's where they got their power. "It applies to all sports, even soccer. I was never taught the importance of the hips until the mid-60's. If I had been taught about using the hips I could have put some guys on the canvas." White won many boxing matches anyway.

When Banks tied Lee in '61, White says he made one of the best calls of his life when he called a short side screen to Bob Tarrant, son of Coach Jimmy Tarrant. The coach's boy scored and Banks went ahead 7-0. Lee came back to score later and the game ended in a tie.

White had been talked into running the same defense that Banks had run the year before, a Dewell Crumpton suggestion. Banks had tied Lee the year before 7-7, a year in which Lee also won the state championship and completed a 8-0-1 season.

White remarks that his team didn't have nearly the players that Lee had but the simple defensive plan, a 6-1 defense with six linemen and one linebacker, worked very effectively against Lee's option. White, of course, kept it simple on offense. He didn't really develop an elaborate offense until the late 60's when his innovative offensive mind took over. But Banks had great defenses throughout the 60's and early 70's.

White says that Tom Jones, the Lee coach, "was in shock," after the game. "He looked like he had lost. White's '61 team finished 5-4. White would play Sidney Lanier the next week in Montgomery. Both Lee and Lanier were powerhouses. "It was suicide playing them back-to-back."

White's all-time favorite assistant coach was Bill Burgess and White had some great ones. Burgess was an assistant on the '65 state championship team; he then took over at Woodlawn in 1966. White remembers going over to Woodlawn to talk to Burgess about football, and walking in on Burgess and Tandy Geralds, Burgess's assistant, engaged in an all-out fight in the locker room. White says they were young and full of vigor. "Those guys were aggressive. They were just having fun. They just wanted to hit somebody so they hit each other. I told 'em to calm down." Burgess beat White in '69, 28-20 when one of White's players was called for holding and a touchdown was called back. The player told White that there was no way he was holding. The score would have put Banks ahead at the time. To White, the film of the play confirmed that his player was right—he didn't hold. White remembers a key play for Woodlawn was when they ran an "88 out of the gate" and former Auburn star David Langner sprinted through the middle of the line all the way for a score.

The '69 team also lost to Alabama High School Hall of Fame coach Bob Finley and Berry 9-7. But White believes the '69 team would have been ready for the playoffs; "We were hot at the end of the season and very well could have won it all. We were licking our chops for the playoffs but we didn't qualify because so few teams made it."

But we are getting ahead of ourselves...

Paige Cutcliffe played for White in '61, '62 and '63 and was one of his finest players, according to White. He played on the offensive line and the defensive line on solid Banks teams that paved the way for White's future success.

Cutcliffe earned a scholarship to play at the University of Florida, where he was a good football player and a superior student. He was a three-time All-Academic player in the SEC and an academic All-American also. At Banks, he was the heavyweight state champion his senior year, wrestling for White, who had started the wrestling program. He also ran track for White. He was one of the bigger runners on the track team when White had him run one of the legs of the mile relay. Once he was exhausted after running a leg in a meet and White shouted, "Go on and get off the track, walrus!"

Cutcliffe started out coaching in high school after college in Florida and spent years struggling with it during the turbulent racial times of the '60s. He didn't pay attention to the color of his players and started five blacks on defense with six whites, and five whites on offense with six blacks. He was driving the basketball team bus in Baker, Florida in the late '60s when his bus got hit by a couple of bricks that smashed the radiator. Cutcliffe called for help from the Central Florida Athletic Office and then took his players to a restaurant to get something to eat. The restaurant worker let him know that whites could eat there but that black players couldn't. Cutcliffe took his team to a 7-11 to get food instead of eating in that restaurant.

Paige got out of coaching and into business. He started a concession business that served Alabama and Auburn football games, then he went on to Coca-Cola where he spent 16 years finishing his career organizing and growing the Eastern Division of the company. Cutcliffe is a master motivational speaker and team builder who still speaks to groups today. He conducts a reading class at a retirement home in Oneonta where he reads books with the elderly. They read classics like *Moby-Dick* and *Tom Sawyer*. His group also read *To Kill a Mockingbird* and the group, every single person, believed that Atticus Finch was right in defending the black man accused in Harper Lee's classic. They also thought Cutcliffe's experience with the Florida restaurant owner was a case of outrageous prejudice. Times have changed for the better.

Cutcliffe is now retired and spends the summer months up in his cabin in Nova Scotia, Canada. He read fourteen books last summer and enjoys the outdoors.

He owes a lot of his drive and success to his high school football coach who he calls, "a man of integrity and a man committed to excellence."

Cutcliffe says the teams were good at Banks, and White "knew how to win, I guarantee you that." But he also thinks that White didn't go overboard in his commitment, though he was highly dedicated to his job. Paige says his brother, David, spends 16-hour days from July to December as offensive coordinator at Tennessee. David assistant coached at Banks for two years in the late '60s and the Jets went 17-3. Paige helped him out in the press box. Paige says that his brother had an uncanny ability to strategize and anticipate when something big was going to happen. "One time he told me we were going to score on the next play and sure enough our running back ran it 80 yards for a touchdown." David has coached some fine players at Tennessee and as former head coach at Ole Miss. He coached Peyton Manning at Tennessee and his younger brother Eli at Ole Miss. Peyton won the Super Bowl in 2007 after calling David the morning of the game. Eli, of course, is carving his career out with the New York Giants. David also coached Heath Shuler, a very successful quarterback at UT, now a congressman from North Carolina. David, who also played for Coach White, has reached thousands of kids, and has made a positive impact in developing his players into better players and more importantly, better people.

That's what Paige says White did at Banks. He had a positive impact on his players' lives. He always reinforced a commitment to excellence in all aspects of his players' lives, and many of his players have gone on to highly successful careers. Cutcliffe mentioned Tommy Thompson, who is a senior vice president of BellSouth, and Bill Jones, the president of O'Neal Steel as examples. White preached excellence in everything you do, according to Cutcliffe, and his drive and enthusiasm for life rubbed off on his players.

"He made a lot of us better people," Cutcliffe adds. "When I saw him at Pleasant Grove in the 90's he was frustrated with some of the kids he had to work with but now I think he is at peace with himself as he looks back on his career. At Banks he worked with kids from middle class America. We wanted to do the right thing. Bobby Johns and I painted his house one time and we thought that was the greatest thing that could happen to us. I washed and scraped dishes. The players cleaned the showers. We were just middle class kids who wanted to work hard and do well for our parents and our coaches."

Ronnie Roddam also played for White in White's early years, graduating in '65. White calls him one of his favorites as Roddam enjoyed great success on the football field at Banks, then at Alabama, lettering in '68 and '69. For thirty-two years, Roddam has worked at Eastern Development Corporation, which manages commercial and multi-family properties. He is currently president.

Roddam remembers White for his toughness on the football field and as a devoted husband and father off the field. "He had high moral values."

Roddam sees White as "a man driven to succeed, and in football that was winning and molding the lives of young people. He ate, slept and drank it. I don't think there is any doubt that he was one of the best high school coaches in Birmingham, Alabama."

Ronnie says that White was truly committed to his job. "He had a tremendous work ethic, whether it was cutting grass, washing jerseys or constantly drawing up X's and O's. He truly studied every aspect of the game, probably in his sleep too."

Roddam played on Banks teams that he described as "solid fundamentally, that loved to hit." They never made the Clinic game when he was there and Roddam says that's because the competition was so fierce with talented, well-coached teams like Woodlawn, Ensley, and Ramsay always in the mix along with Banks. But White was the master motivator, according to Roddam, who never lost focus on getting 100 percent out of his players and molding them into the best players and people they could be.

"If you screwed up and did something really stupid off the field, he didn't mind putting the paddle to you. Teachers and coaches could get away with that in those days."

Roddam shares two stories etched in his memory from his playing days at Banks:

"The week before each game we would watch film of our upcoming opponent. In '64 we were playing Vigor High School at Samford's field. All week before the game Coach White would warn us that we'd better not be tiptoeing around or number 55 would take a cheap shot at us. Well, number 55 was a guy by the name of Steve Bigelow and he did love to blind-side players. Late in the first half I saw number 55 tiptoeing around. He never saw me coming and I absolutely nailed him right about the time the whistle blew. Of course the referee threw a flag and penalized us. Coach White yanked me out of the game and sent me to the locker room early. I didn't get back in the game until midway into the third quarter. To this day I blame Coach White for the penalty because all he could talk about the week of the game was number 55.

"That same year we were playing Walker County High School in Jasper. We were 4-0 at the time and thought we would kick their country rear ends and head on back to the big city. Boy, were we in for a surprise. On the way to the game the team bus stopped at a little restaurant outside Jasper where Coach White had arranged a pre-game meal. He cautioned us not to eat too much. Well, when he turned his back we pigged out. Lots of biscuits, butter and honey. We were stuffed. When we arrived at the field to play, the managers for Walker County took us into our dressing room. We were accustomed to playing our games at Legion Field and their facilities were a joke compared to what we were used to. The managers overheard some of our players making fun of their dressing room and reported it to their head coach, D. Joe Gambrell.

I found out later that Coach Gambrell had tears in his eyes before the game and told his team we were making fun of them. Coach White could sense we weren't thrilled to be there and warned us we better get our minds on the game. Well, it was too late. They beat us in every phase of the game. Those were the meanest and toughest guys I have ever played against. They would pinch and bite you in a pile-up. Jerry Colvin, a successful attorney here in Birmingham, was the quarterback on that Walker County team and he and I still laugh about the lesson they taught us."

But that was an aberration for Banks. White was always ready to play and so were his teams the majority of the time. For Ronnie Roddam, the experience under White is one he will always remember:

"I feel like one of the luckiest people in the world to have come along when I did. I didn't realize it until later in life just how much Coach White meant to me. I've always been disappointed that Coach White has not yet gotten in the Alabama High School Hall of Fame. He certainly deserves to be in there. I love him."

CHAPTER 9
Breakthrough (1965)

White always had physical battles with Woodlawn. He calls those games "some of the hardest-hitting games I was ever involved in. Head knockers. Woodlawn really had head hunters." White's teams were pretty hard-hitting too. It was a fierce rivalry.

Banks defeated Woodlawn 21-6 in the '63 season. The Jets, as usual, were playing the Colonels in basketball the following winter. The coaches from Banks would go to the Banks-Woodlawn basketball game and the Woodlawn coaches would go to their games against Banks.

One of the students for Banks who was working the scoreboard put in the score of the football game on the scoreboard at halftime. Woodlawn Coach Johnny Howell was at the game as was White. White looked over, saw Howell's face and knew he was angry. So was White.

"I could see by his face that he didn't appreciate it," White says. "I didn't either."

White went down and took the score off the board.

The next year White believes Woodlawn had extra incentive to beat Banks because of the scoreboard incident. Woodlawn won the football game 20-14. "They had something to feed on," White says. "The kid who did it wasn't an athlete. They beat us but not by much. It was the most physical game I had ever seen. It was similar to the '74 game even though there was not as much talent on the field. It was a war."

White asserts that the blocking when he was coaching was a lot more physical than it is today. When he was at Banks, players used their whole bodies to block.

"It was explosive. You would drive with your legs and put your whole body into the defensive player. You would use your headgear and your shoulder pads. If the play was going to the right and the blocker was on the left side he would get on the inside of his man. We weren't as big but we were probably quicker than they are today. They're big and strong today at places like Hoover and they use their hands more with the spread formations. They power block on the runs. You couldn't use your hands back then."

White taught summer school at West End in '64.

"Those kids were harassing me in history class about playing us the next year and beating us. They told me they wanted me to wear a pair of orange socks to the game. I bought a pair and wore them the next year at the game. I had told the kids that every time we scored a touchdown, I'd roll my britches up and show the socks. We beat 'em the next year and every time we scored I'd look across the field and roll up my pants a little bit to show the socks. I was wondering who would be looking from their sideline. You had to have a little fun out there."

White knew that after the '64 season, he had the material coming back to have a stellar '65 season. White, gathering his sophomores together after a practice in '63, had challenged them:

"If you guys stick together, follow the weight program and take football seriously, we will go undefeated and win the state championship."

In the first game of the '65 season, White's team beat Bessemer 7-0 with a goal-line stand. "We were a little unsure of ourselves at the time."

The next week the Jets shut out Ensley 13-0. "We got a little better. The next week we beat Walker 28-0 and really got better."

In that Walker game, the defense did not allow Walker to get past the 50-yard line the whole game, until in the last few minutes, when Walker got to the 10. White told his defense they'd better stop 'em. Three plays later Walker was at the 20 and never scored.

The Jets beat Ramsay 19-6, and Berry 33-0. Mike Kolen, who starred at Auburn and with the Miami Dolphins, earning the name Captain Crunch, talks with White about it to this day. He always says "Coach, y'all took us to the woodshed."

Banks then beat West End 14-0. In the first six games, the Jets' defense had only allowed six points.

The next week was Woodlawn and White expected and got a hotly contested game decided in the last minutes. Down 14-13, Banks drove the ball down the field behind the outstanding blocking of the line and the running of fullback Bruce Lindsay. Lindsay was the leading rusher for Banks that year. With a third down on the Woodlawn 35, White called a screen pass to sophomore Johnny Musso, the tailback.

Musso caught the pass and ran it down to the 10-yard line. White then called Musso's number again. White wanted a power run off tackle. Musso ran for the hole, saw it stopped up, and bounced outside for the flag. At the five-yard line Musso left his feet and dove all the way into the end zone. Banks had to stop a late Woodlawn drive to win the game 20-14.

"I gave Johnny a highlight film of his Banks career," White says. "He doesn't know where it is. That's the only time I've ever been disappointed in him."

The rest of the season Banks rolled. They beat Phillips 40-6, Jones Valley 22-10 and Ramsay again, 7-0. They scored 203 points and had six shutouts on defense. Twice they gave up six points and they gave up 10 to Jones Valley and 14 to Woodlawn.

The Jets finished the season 10-0 and were voted state champions by the sportswriters across the state. This with a highly competitive schedule—every team that the Jets played was a test. White's prediction to his sophomores two years before was true. The man knew his football teams.

For White, it was a memorable group with multiple players going to the college ranks.

Larry Gunnin was the starting defensive end. Jeff Masters, the starting linebacker went to Samford. Ken Wahlers went to Auburn. Kirk Stallings went to Mississippi State. Danny Cooper went Division II. Sam Chambliss moved to wing back his senior year and went on to play free safety at Tennessee. Billy Strickland, one of White's warriors, played defensive end and tackle. Strickland played at Alabama. Johnny Johnston played defensive tackle and running back. Johnston went on to Alabama. Mike Pitts went to The Citadel.

Johnny Musso was the best running back on the team but White wanted Johnston to get a scholarship so he played Johnston more, as Musso was just a sophomore. Musso became an All-American at Alabama and has been inducted into the College Football Hall of Fame.

Rhett Wood was a defensive tackle. "What a football player," White says. Wood went to Samford on scholarship.

Lindsay played in college. White says it was either West Alabama or North Alabama.

Ronnie Massey was a nose guard and offensive guard; he went to Tennessee on scholarship. Allan Girardeau played linebacker and offensive guard for White. He went to Auburn. Don Roberts, who White says, "looked like a football player" got hurt but would have been a key player on a good college team.

Merrill Mann was the quarterback and he went to Jacksonville

State. Mann was a straight A student to boot. Phil Cochran was a sophomore center, nose guard and linebacker. "Anywhere we put him he was outstanding," White recalls.

John Easley was a key player. Rusty Morrow was the long snapper and a standout basketball player. He went on to play football and basketball at Arkansas. Larry Willingham, a junior, could play anywhere. White played him in the secondary, defensive end and sometimes at running back. "Anytime somebody got hurt, here comes Larry!" White says. "I should have left him at running back. He was so fast. He could burn it." Willingham went on to star at Auburn and play for the St. Louis Cardinals, where he was a standout cornerback.

The second Ramsay game was one of the toughest games of the season. Ramsay was coached by legend Mutt Reynolds and there was a lot of mutual respect between the head coaches of the teams and the assistants. White called a play where Allan Girardeau was supposed to pull and trap Tommy Yearout, Ramsay's outstanding tackle. "I told Allan we were going to trap Yearout and you're going to pull and probably make the hardest hit in the football game. After contact, Yearout ran to the sideline holding his shoulder and Allan had a big gash on his nose. Both came back in the game. That shows how tough they were." That was the Clinic game and Banks won it 7-0 to close out the season.

White remarks that this was his most memorable team. "Not only were they good athletes, a couple great, it was their attitude and their character. It was the way their parents raised them. They were outstanding students. Many of those kids enjoyed success in the business world. Several are now millionaires.

"They were fun to coach. I looked forward to going to practice. They would do whatever you asked them to do without questioning you."

White had a top-flight staff as well: Bill Burgess, one of his favorites of all time, Don Green, also a favorite, and Bill Lankford, who coached the B team.

"The thing I liked about Bill Lankford was his patience," White says. "He was a real good, sincere person. He has remained that way. He was also an outstanding basketball coach."

White got so much accomplished in the '65 season despite so much unrest throughout the country and at Banks associated with the Vietnam War.

"It was a depressing time. The country was spiraling out of control. Thank God for football. There were all kinds of demonstrations. It made you sick to your stomach. When I watched TV I got so mad I had to turn it off. That's the way it is now. The population has gotten too soft."

White remembers when the Japanese bombed Pearl Harbor; he was glued to the radio. He thinks Franklin Roosevelt was both a good war-time and peace-time president. "There was so much unity then. I wonder how Roosevelt would fare today."

White has mixed emotions about Lyndon Johnson, president during most of the Vietnam War. White believes he was hiding information from the American people and he didn't like that. "You have to be honest with the people of this country. The people should run the country. The president should be up front and stay honest. Johnson was too secretive. He may have been doing what he thought was right but you've got to open it up to the people."

White is a believer in setting a firm course and sticking with it. He doesn't want America to cut and run from its battles. He never surrendered. That is one of the main reasons he was successful. He remains a patriotic American who believes in the value of the work ethic, standing by principle and seeing everything through. He still expects that in others, particularly in his country's leaders.

A favorite leader to Shorty was his assistant coach, Bill Burgess, who went on to have multiple successes as a high school and college football coach, first at Woodlawn and Oxford High Schools where his squads were perennial playoff teams; and then at Jacksonville State where he won the Division II National Championship in 1992 after having taken his team to two other National Championship games.

Burgess says he developed a good bit of his philosophy on coaching from Coach White whom he was an assistant for at Banks from '63-'66. Burgess was fresh out of Auburn when White hired him to coach linebackers, tight ends and wide receivers. Burgess and White formed a bond that they will always cherish. They are still great friends today.

"We were highly compatible," White notes. "I had two coaches [Don Green being the other one] and we had to do it all [White was the offensive and defensive coordinator]. Bill adapted well. He's one of my favorites."

Burgess's affable personality reminds me a lot of White. They worked very well together and formed a lasting friendship. Burgess thinks White could excel today.

"He's still got it," he says of White. "If he went back into coaching today he'd win. I was very fortunate because the first job I had right out of college was with him. He gave me a lot of responsibilities. He was a very hard worker and he taught us how to work hard.

"He was a big technique guy. He was ahead of his time. Most of the philosophies I developed concerning football I learned from him."

Burgess is adamant that along with being a great teacher, White demanded respect for team rules amongst his players. There were no compromises in what White believed in and what he exemplified.

"He demanded discipline from his players to his coaches. But he was there for you and would back you up. He'd also get on you." Bill noticed that White developed a great chemistry with his players as they matured in the program.

"I think the longer our players were at Banks the more he cared about them. He'd fuss at you but at the same time he'd do anything to help you."

To Burgess, White hasn't changed one iota.

"God knows he's the same guy I used to work for at Banks. He's still got that fire. He has that same bounce in his walk. I was fortunate to have worked under him."

Burgess says that White's attention to detail was precise, down to towels in their proper place, equipment neatly placed in lockers, immaculate coaches' offices and the practice field.

"He would take care of all the little things. After Friday night games we'd be in there Saturday morning washing clothes. At other places mommas were washing them.

"He never asked you to be at a practice or a meeting unless he was there himself."

Burgess also says that White was a master preparation coach. That's how he motivated his coaches and his troops. His military discipline helped him immensely.

"The biggest motivator for him was being prepared. It gave everybody the confidence to play 110 percent. He'd also talk to you and have that left hand moving and have you ready to play. He was going to have his team prepared.

"He made you believe. He took the stuff you did well and got it out of you. He was a master at Banks High School of making the team believe they would win. Not that they might win but truly believe they would win." Burgess played the good guy at practice many times, as the head man would jump on his players if he thought practice wasn't going according to plan.

"He'd get on you no doubt about it, but later he'd come up to you and put his arm around you and say something positive to you."

Bill Burgess played a key role in the '65 state championship team as voted on by the writers in the Birmingham area.

"We practiced hard and we played hard. It was a special group."

White kept telling me that many of those players went on to become major successes in business with quite a few becoming multi-millionaires.

"It was a typical Shorty White team, committed to excellence," Burgess recalls.

To Burgess, White was a genius at teaching footwork for his linemen. Bill also says there was no grey area on who was calling the shots.

"Don and I had a great relationship with him, we'd have fun and kid around with him, but when he got that left hand going we knew to shut up and listen. There wasn't any doubt who was boss." And Burgess still has a lot of admiration for his good friend and mentor.

"I love to see him and run into him at different places. He's a great guy to be around. Again, he could go back tomorrow and win. Football is blocking and tackling and he taught that better than anybody else." White had all the tools the great coaches possess, according to Burgess, who went on to carve out a great career himself at Woodlawn from '67-'70, at Oxford from '71-'84, then at Jax State for 12 years.

White loves to recount the time when he walked into Burgess's office in Woodlawn when Burgess and assistant coach Tandy Geralds were having an intense wrestling match in the locker room. They were friends having a friendly bout.

"They were in their early 30's and full of energy. I went in there and said, 'Hey y'all break that up.' I was afraid they were going to hurt each other. They were having a ball!"

And what a job Burgess did in '71 when his team won three ballgames in a week. Due to postponement of a couple of games early in the season, Woodlawn had to play Ensley on a Friday night, Ramsay the following Monday and Banks the next Friday. He defeated White that next Friday, one of the few times Woodlawn beat Banks, 28-20 on a freezing night.

White believes if Woodlawn hadn't had to play those three regular-season games in a week at the end of the season that the Colonels would have won the state championship. They lost in the first round to Robert E. Lee of Montgomery.

"I try not to get wrapped up in 'what if,'" Burgess says. "Football is the greatest sport in that it teaches you so much. It was a lot of work but our players didn't care, they just wanted to play. Those rascals didn't think about it at all."

One of the most dedicated of Shorty White's rascals was Billy Strickland, now 58 years old. Billy is not one to revel in his high school and college football accomplishments; he doesn't live in the past. He's been very successful in the metals business and had a great run on the commodities floor in Chicago in the '80s, where he worked with former teammate Johnny Musso. He doesn't like it when athletes live in the past, and he is focused only on the present, growing his metals business that has stretched out to Albany, Georgia and Dothan, Alabama among other sites.

But when asked about his playing days at Banks where he won a state championship in 1965 under Shorty White and his college career where he played for Bear Bryant, an undeniable legend, Strickland freely states his opinions about each man and their views on football and life.

Strickland was an outstanding defensive end for White and an offensive lineman his senior year for Bryant when he battled with Pro Football Hall of Famer John Hannah for a starting guard position. Hannah was later named by *Sports Illustrated* as the greatest NFL offensive lineman ever, playing for the New England Patriots.

"Big John gave a speech at the Touchdown Club in which he remembered struggling his sophomore year and Coach Bryant all over him as he was battling it out with a senior. He was talking about me. I was real proud of that," Strickland says.

Strickland had never had anyone in his family play sports and the first college game he saw was during his junior year at Banks when the Alabama coaches gave his friend Johnny Johnston and his older brother, Donnie, tickets to the game. Donnie was being recruited by Alabama for football.

Billy started in basketball but was cut from the freshman team and Johnston told him if he didn't go out for the football team he was chicken.

Strickland says that he was from the old school in his work ethic and that White was from "the older school." "There's old school and I guess there may even be an older school, but I'm certain that Coach White was from the Oldest School…White expected hard work and dedication and would accept nothing less.

"There was an article in the paper about kids today being pampered and playing in all these summer camps and if things don't go their way and they don't have a loving bond with their coach they quit."

Strickland and his teammates at Banks didn't have that experience. Quitting wasn't an option. It was about playing for the team in a selfless manner, for a tough, determined coach who would push you to the limit to test your fortitude. It seemed to work out pretty well for Strickland and his teammates.

Strickland says that going from Banks to Alabama was not a major transition because he was used to a system that was very organized and had many gut checks to test one's mettle. Strickland thinks Alabama was more intense because of the quality of the athletes in larger numbers, but he learned the value of the work ethic from Shorty White. It was only intensified by Bear Bryant.

"He was a tremendously talented high school coach," Strickland says. "One of my pet peeves is athletes who don't get on with their lives, they only want to talk about the old days. Coach Bryant did have a tremendous influence on my life. My father died my senior year at Banks and I was a cocky high school athlete. Coach Bryant's discipline and work ethic were exactly what I needed. It helped me tremendously but I think Coach White laid the foundation for that."

Strickland still doesn't call his former coach "Shorty" just as he would have never have called Paul Bryant, "Bear." White is Coach White and Bryant, Coach Bryant.

Strickland remembers 1965 vividly as when there were still no black high school athletes for the most part in Alabama. But Strickland believes that White could have related to any player regardless of the color of his skin.

"It wouldn't matter if you were black, white or Hispanic, if you gave Coach White everything you had he would rejoice in your successes. And, by golly, he wouldn't cut you any slack no matter who you were."

Billy says he played for a coach in high school who had tunnel vision when it came to his job.

"It was his life. You talk to June and his kids and they probably paid the price to a degree because he was there early in the morning and late at night and on the weekends watching film and preparing. It appeared to us that he was very intense about it. He's like a Dick Vermeil. He loved his players but it was very, very frustrating for him when they didn't do what he wanted them to do. He'd challenge you, scream at you and push you to the limit, but you knew at the end of the day that he cared about you. He cared about you as an individual and where you were going and what he was teaching you."

Strickland points to White's honesty as one of his most notable characteristics:

"He was very opinionated about what you were supposed to do and in most instances he was right. I get confused whether it was Coach Bryant or Coach White who said it. Both said the same thing that nothing in life is worthwhile that you'll achieve that doesn't involve a lot of hard work, blood, sweat and probably some tears. You don't build character by having mommy and daddy fixing it for you. You build character by finding out when you're out there one-on-one in a gut check and nobody can help you and the coach is screaming at you. Did we know we were learning those lessons at 17-18 years old? No. But looking back that's what Coach White's philosophy was."

Strickland believes that his '65 team was very talented. There were Division One players on the team. But the '64 team was considered to be White's best. The '64 team lost the last game of the season and so had a disappointing year. Strickland says the seniors were crying in the showers after the last game. The juniors got together and decided they were not going to have that happen to them. The juniors had a meeting that spring and decided to commit themselves to winning and doing things the right way. One of the younger players—a talented one—had been out drinking and seniors called him in to warn him he was not going to do that on their watch.

"We just had a great group of guys," Strickland says. "You know how you have a bad class one year and a great class the next. Well, we had a great group. We had different personalities but we worked well together."

Strickland emphasizes that what was awesome about the '65 team was the defense. "I bet we were in the offensive backfield eight out of ten times. Coach White had us doing things that no other high school team was doing. I wouldn't want to have played us. Johnny Johnston had film for us at a get-together we had and we had guys making big plays who weren't great athletes."

Strickland is proud of the talent his Banks championship team had. Larry Willingham was an All-American at Auburn and then played for the St. Louis Cardinals, Musso was an All-American at Alabama, Johnston signed with Alabama, Strickland signed at Alabama, Allan Girardeau signed with Auburn, Merrill Mann signed with Jacksonville State, Jeff Masters inked with Samford, and Sam Chambliss signed with Tennessee.

"It was the combination of us having the horses, good coaching and we had a lot of things go our way that led to a championship."

Strickland says these were kids from working class families in East Lake and Roebuck that started turning heads in the stands and in the newspaper.

"I noticed when I knocked somebody down everybody was liking me and I had a lot of friends. I think we all figured that out and thrived on it. All of a sudden you have people putting your picture in the paper and coaches calling you. My dad worked for the railroad. Coach Bryant and Shug Jordan were calling my dad by his first name and taking him to dinner at The Club and Dale's Steakhouse. I was thinking, 'We need to keep this up.'"

Strickland believes that White was somewhere in between a coach focused on winning at all costs, like Bryant was, and a coach out there to teach his kids values of sportsmanship and fair play and win a few ballgames. Strickland sees similarities between White and Rush Propst in their intensity levels, but also believes that White was totally dedicated to his players. He had that Bryant-General Patton attitude, but he did care about his players' well-being.

White's tenure at Alabama ('75-'81) was frustrating for him, thinks Strickland.

"I don't think Coach Bryant respected Coach White's enthusiasm. Coach White always called the shots in high school. He would say to Bryant and the coaches down there, you got to try this and nobody would listen to him. I don't think they had a great love for one another. It's not unusual. I don't think General Patton and General Westmoreland would have gotten along well. But I think Coach White in his element was one of the great high school coaches, certainly in the state and probably in the country."

Strickland says that Bryant would tell his players, "By God you better win or you don't want to practice on Monday." He was not the nice-guy head coach that Shug Jordan at Auburn was labeled as, though Strickland says that was an undeserved label. "Coach Jordan was a tough son of a gun."

Strickland says that White was "much more on the intense side. He wanted you to do everything you could to win and everything you could to prepare to win. He wanted your very best and would tolerate nothing less."

But Strickland points out that White and Bryant were similar in their ability to take average players and make them good players, and take good players and make them great players. "He'd take a player who didn't know he wasn't good and gave it 150 percent and make him a good player." Players who were not stars on the '65 team contributed by making big plays on both sides of the ball.

Strickland says that White told his '65 team after they won the state championship that the '64 team had much more talent but they didn't have the heart of the '65 team.

"I have three daughters and my youngest one played basketball for Fran Braasch at Vestavia. Fran is one of my all-time favorite coaches. She told me one time that the world is full of talented, unsuccessful people.

"That was one of Coach White's pet peeves. He would rather coach a kid who really wasn't that good but who would leave his heart on the field than a kid with all the talent who would only give 75 percent because he thought he was cool. Coach Bryant and Coach White would take a kid who was not as good as the kid in front of him but by the fourth quarter the kid was busting his guts out."

Could White be successful today with a different attitude from some kids who would not respond as well to White's fierce approach in driving his players?

"I think so. I refer back to Vestavia and Sammy Dunn. Sammy was a Coach White clone, 25 years later in baseball." Dunn won state championships in baseball at Vestavia in '88 and eight out of nine years from 1991-2000.

"Sammy could do it at Vestavia with a bunch of rich kids. You would think the parents wouldn't stand for it, the yelling at his players and the midnight practices. But kids really want a challenge. He was genuine like Coach White was and kids respond to that. Coach White didn't have the best bedside manner with the parents, but the kids responded to him. He would do anything for the kid that gave him everything he had."

And White had a tender side.

"When my dad died my senior year in high school, Coach White came to my house physically and stayed with my mother. He didn't have to say anything. He wasn't there because he felt he needed to be there or had to be there. He knew in his heart he had to be there."

White was there for Strickland again when Strickland got into some trouble at Alabama his junior year.

"I was having a bad day at practice. I was practicing with a dislocated shoulder and Richard Williamson [an assistant—Bryant was not at practice that day] came up to me after practice and got into my face and started grabbing my facemask. I told him in an impolite way to quit doing it and he did it again so I backhanded him or hit him and knocked him down. The coaches came up to me and grabbed me and kicked me off the field. "We were talking and laughing about it in the dorm that night when the dorm coach called me and told me Coach Bryant wanted to see me at 5 a.m. the next morning.

He told me the next day that he was glad I decided to quit and that there were some younger players he was looking at. I told Coach I was not going to quit, but he told me that I just needed to concentrate on my schoolwork and talk to him in a couple of months. I drove away and was crying like a baby.

"Coach White went down there—I didn't know this until 15 or 20 years later when my mother told me—and talked to Coach Bryant and told him that he knew me and knew my heart and knew I was a winner."

Bryant eventually let Strickland come back and their relationship changed after that. Strickland was a captain for a couple of games his senior year. Because Bryant saw that fire in Strickland from what happened on the practice field, he started really liking him.

"He told me, 'Billy I want you to start competing with this young lineman we've got, Hannah, and find out if he's any good.' He also told me one time at Legion Field that he wanted me to try some shoes on the turf to see if they would work for me. Our relationship totally changed after that situation with Richard Williamson. I wish I had done it my freshman year."

Strickland finished his career at Alabama then went down to New Orleans to try out for the Saints. He injured his knee and came back to Birmingham to work in the banking business. He gave it another shot with the Saints the next year but injuries prevented him from making the team. He's now in the recycling business in metals and making a good living in that field. He had been in Chicago, working with his good friend Johnny Musso in the '80s and was highly successful on the commodities floor. Billy was making a solid six-figure salary and says that Musso was making a seven-figure salary.

"He was an All-American at Alabama and he was an All-American on the Board of Trade. He is the most tender-hearted man you would ever want to meet but he makes a 180 when he is on the football field or in a competitive arena. He's a warrior."

Musso is an avid golfer who plays to a nine handicap. Strickland says he is one of the best athletes he's ever been around.

"Whatever he sets out to do, he does it well. Joe Namath was like that. One time we were playing basketball in a pickup game and Namath was under the basket and jumped up and dunked with two hands behind his head. This was in '66. Johnny was like that."

Strickland now spends time with his wife, and daughters when they're home—they're all out of the house—and flies for a hobby.

"I don't like golf a lot, but I fly World War II planes and I've got a Beech Bonanza. Johnny Musso has been up with me. I fly the most famous World War II plane, the P-51 Mustang."

Strickland is one of White's players who not only succeeded for him on the football field but also has been a huge success in business. White says that's what he is most proud of about his '65 team. Strickland's final thought about his strict coach:

"One thing about Coach White is when his and Jimmy Sidle's mom died, he took Jimmy in and there was no question he was going to do that. That speaks volumes about him."

A Strickland teammate, Allan Girardeau was a linebacker anchoring the '65 defense that allowed only 36 points in 10 games, under four points a game with six shutouts. Girardeau went on to earn a football scholarship at Auburn and is now in the insurance business in Birmingham.

He remembers the '65 team as committed to the purpose of being a winner after the disappointing '64 team went 5-4 after having been predicted to be the best team in the state at the beginning of that season. Girardeau was a member of a special senior class helped by a talented underclassman in Johnny Musso, a sophomore at the time.

After beating Bessemer in their first game 7-0 and then Ensley 13-0, Banks went to work under White's leadership. According to Girardeau, White apologized for not having them ready for the Ensley game and he made them do 100-yard runs that Monday. It never seemed to end. Girardeau found it very tough, but it made the team stronger physically and mentally and was a key part of pushing the '65 team, which went undefeated and won the state, White's first of three state titles.

"Coach White was always pushing us but he never cussed at us or grabbed our facemasks," Allan remembers. "He knew what it took to motivate different people. Some guys he would pat on the back all the time and some other guys he would yell at if he felt he needed to. With Musso he always patted him on the back because Johnny never did anything wrong!"

Girardeau also said White was great in games.

"He was really good at making adjustments. He used Merrill Mann at quarterback and Merrill was a very smart guy. He was probably a better linebacker than quarterback. He could hit you. But Mann was great at making adjustments and picking up tendencies of the defense. He had a great head on his shoulders."

Girardeau said there were no huge guys on the team. Billy Strickland was a 6-4, 205-pound offensive lineman who went on to have great success at Alabama. Ronnie Massey was around 200 on the line. Musso weighed 165 dripping wet. Larry Willingham was a split end who became an All-American at Auburn and played many years for the St. Louis Cardinals in the NFL. Girardeau said a 220 to 230-pound player in the city football system was "a rarity."

Girardeau calls Musso "a great athlete," who played basketball, baseball, wrestled and ran track. It wasn't unusual for Musso to have a track meet, then have a baseball game or a wrestling match that night. As for White, Girardeau echoes many of his former teammates— he was by the book in his discipline and there were no exceptions to his rules.

"From what I've been told there was a German on our team who would drink beer with his family at night and Coach White caught wind of it. He kicked him off the team. He would have been a great player, probably an SEC-caliber player, but Coach White would not put up with that. He wanted all of his boys to make a good appearance and he wasn't going to put up with that. He wanted us to be gentlemen in public and abide by training rules."

Allan remembers when White had the players out on the field picking up rocks as he was trying to get the practice field in mint condition in '64. "We started throwing rocks and Coach White got the coaches together and they came out and he told us we were going to have to run a six-minute mile. It was five laps around the field and on the first lap a lot of us ran 45 seconds. Coach White had a stopwatch and he said that we were going to set a world record when we passed him on the first lap. When we got halfway through our second lap everybody hit the wall. We ran the mile in around 6:30 and Coach White said we would have to come out the next day and run it again. Well, a lot of the guys skipped school and luckily Coach White forgot about it."

For Girardeau, the rivalry with Woodlawn was huge as there was not a Huffman or an Erwin yet in the area. In '65 Banks won 20-14 in what Girardeau called a very hard-hitting game. Larry Gunnin, a defensive back, intercepted a pass and ran it back for a touchdown. Musso dove across the goal line for another touchdown. It was a memorable game in that hard-fought rivalry.

Girardeau declares White a true legend, one of the best high school coaches who ever competed.

"He deserves to be in the Hall of Fame. You see many of these coaches who are in and Coach White's record is just as good. He deserves some sort of recognition."

Hopefully he will get it.

Another man with strong feelings about Shorty White's accomplishments is Jeff Masters, a standout linebacker/tight end for White from '63-'65. He was a major impact player on the state championship team in '65. He and his teammates had gathered together in '64 after the team suffered through a not-so-successful season and the principal had told White he would be fired, letting Shorty know this in the locker room after a game.

The players, Masters one of them, banded together after White left the locker room and decided they were not going to allow White to be fired. They marched to the principal's office the next day.

"We had told each other that the reason we hadn't won is because we didn't do what Coach White wanted us to do and that was give 110 percent. We were picked to be an outstanding team by the papers that year and we turned out to be mediocre. We knew it was our own doing. We went to the principal's office the next day and told him that if Shorty White goes, we go too! It was going to be tough to field a football team if we were not going to play. How could you fire one of the best high school coaches that ever lived?"

Masters and his teammates' move paid off in a huge way as the next year Banks dominated football in the city and the state. They went 10-0 scoring 203 points and only allowing 36; that's just over three points a game with six shutouts. White showed he was one of the elite coaches in the state. He proved later how good he was with more state championships and a solid, character-filled group of players who played tough, hard-nosed football while being supremely coached.

Jeff remembers playing Woodlawn in '65 at Legion Field with more than 20,000 people in attendance. It was a renewal of the top rivalry in the state and Banks of course won 20-14. Woodlawn and Banks were both undefeated at the time.

Masters says that every starter on the '65 team received a college football scholarship offer, a testament to White as a coach and to his top assistant Bill Burgess.

For Jeff, the most interesting thing he learned from teammate Johnny Johnston was that Coach Bryant would recruit players from Banks and other schools, and if the players were equal in talent Bryant would take the player from the other school, because he didn't think he could teach the Banks player anything that he didn't already know! Of course many Banks players did play at Alabama and were very successful in Tuscaloosa.

Masters is proud that not only were the seniors highly successful on the next level but that underclassmen Johnny Musso and Larry Willingham were future All-Americans in college football.

Jeff went on to play football at Samford, taking his hard-nosed, dedicated and knowledgeable approach to the collegiate level.

"Samford would sign a lot more players than they had an allotment for and they would boil it down over the summer," Masters says, noting that Samford was not a Division One school and didn't have restrictions on the amount of players signed. "I went up against this 300-pound tackle in drills and was whipping him and he stood up after I knocked him on his tail and whined, 'Coach, he's cheating.' I was merely using the technique Bill Burgess had taught me at Banks for getting low and going under the opponent's sternum. The Samford coaches didn't teach that. I had been taught the right technique for playing my position."

Masters confirms—like all the other players who played for White—that White was tough, no-nonsense and a strict disciplinarian.

"He would get on you hard but he would always give you constructive criticism after he got on you. He wanted perfection and he pushed you to the limit to make you a successful player. If you didn't give him 100 percent you'd get the paddle, or worse, he might kick you off the team."

Masters's mentor White was dedicated to his players as people more than anything else. Of course he wanted to win and he did that in a big way, but White was concerned greatly about his players' achievement and advancement in life.

"He was a good man, he didn't forget us. He didn't get the credit he deserves for getting us scholarships. He always contacted schools, trying to get us scholarships. He personally cared about us."

Certainly White motivated young Jeff through his actions and through his words.

"Was I motivated? Hell yes I was motivated. It's hard to define. You just saw him working his tail off to make you a better player. He would not raise Cain without giving you some constructive criticism. There were coaches later who would curse me but not show me how to do it right. He always did."

And Masters marvels that White's motivation for doing things the right way hasn't changed.

"He looks and acts today like the day I met him. He is energetic in everything he says and does. He's never been one to prop his feet up. His coaches Don Green and Bill Burgess went on to college coaching and Bill Burgess had a lot of success on the collegiate level at Jacksonville State where he won a national championship in '92 and took his teams to three national championship games from '88-'92, posting a 56-8-1 record in those years. It shows how Coach White could choose the best coaches."

Masters says that the '65 team never ran up the score against their opponents because White was against doing that. He was all about creating a lasting team chemistry.

"We recently had a reunion at the Alabama Sports Hall of Fame and guys from all over the place, different states, came back for it. The camaraderie on that team exists today."

That sentiment of togetherness is echoed by Johnny Johnston, a key member of White's '65 state championship team at Banks, Shorty's first state title as a head coach and the foundation for some stellar years at Banks. Johnston says there were no superstars on the team, just a bunch of blue-collar kids willing to make the sacrifice it took to succeed mightily on the football field and in the classroom.

There was one standout on the team, Sam Chambliss, who Johnston says could have been a big-time college football player. Grades kept him back. Chambliss was the state decathlon winner and a standout defensive back on the football team. But there were many very good players. Johnny Musso was a sophomore and Johnston says, "You could tell he was going to be something special."

Johnny says that White had tunnel vision with his football team. He wanted them to go undefeated and win a state championship. White had gotten his players into lifting weights in '64 and the work was beginning to pay off.

"Nobody was real fancy, we were a close-knit team," he says. "We believed what Coach White told us and played probably above our heads sometimes. We won with defense."

That defense pitched six shutouts and only allowed 36 points in 10 games. "Nobody could score on us, we had eight or ten goal-line stands. We were a bunch of kids who believed what Coach White told us and did what he asked us to do."

Johnny calls Merrill Mann, the quarterback of that Jets team, a "Pat Trammell-type player. He was not going to get you beat."

Johnston says that most of the players played both ways. He was a tailback at the beginning of the season but tore cartilage in his knee and was out until game four. "Johnny took over and it was not difficult to see what Johnny Musso was going to be like. He made clutch plays, big plays."

Johnston also played nose guard for White. There were some players who were standouts like center Phil Cochran, a 175-pound sophomore, and Billy Strickland, who along with Johnston played at Alabama. Strickland was a 205-pound tackle along with Ronnie Massey. Larry Gunnin and Jeff Masters were standouts too on defense. Masters was a notorious tough guy according to White. He played linebacker. Bruce Lindsey was a solid 185-pound fullback. Allan Girardeau and Rhett Wood were the offensive guards.

Massey went to Tennessee, Masters to Samford. Chambliss averaged 40 yards a punt also. He signed with Tennessee but ended up at Samford.

Asked if the '65 team was a group of overachievers, Johnston says,

"We definitely didn't underachieve."

And Johnston says a lot of it had to do with their head coach.

"He was a very strict disciplinarian. You knew you couldn't get by with anything. We trusted him and had confidence in what he told us. We didn't always like him. We do now.

"As freshmen and sophomores we didn't feel close to him. When we were seniors we did. The purpose of a coach is not to be your friend but to be your coach. We respected him and tried to give him everything we had."

And White was a taskmaster.

"He would push us to the limit and beyond the limit," Johnston says. "Some teams couldn't handle being pushed like that, but we did. We were middle class kids who didn't mind working hard and believed in what he told us."

And White had Bill Burgess on his staff.

"Everybody was crazy about Bill Burgess," Johnston says. "He was a fantastic coach. He coached defensive ends and linebackers. Don Green was a good coach too. They were both real young assistant coaches."

And Johnston adds that beyond football, White taught his players about life.

"He always emphasized character. He talked about character and a relationship with God, your parents and your teammates."

Johnston remembers a particular game against Woodlawn in the undefeated state championship '65 season that stood out to him. Woodlawn, of course, was Banks's biggest rival. There was a real dislike there. Woodlawn had scored to go ahead with six minutes left in the game. Johnston returned the kickoff to the 35 and got tackled and re-injured his knee. As Musso was running off the field, Johnston hollered at him that he was going to have to play tailback. "It was the biggest game of our lives and we were down by a point. Bruce Lindsey got most of the carries on the drive.

"It was third or fourth down with two yards to go inside their 10. Coach called a running play to the tailback off tackle and Johnny hit the line of scrimmage."

The line was stacked up so Musso ran outside. He scored.

"It was one of the greatest runs I've ever seen," White remembers. "He got to the five-yard line and he went airborne. He was hit by two defenders but he made it to the end zone. Boom!"

Banks won the game 20-14 and completed a perfect season with wins over Jones Valley and Ramsay the following two weeks.

Johnston says he talks to White today. "Other than my father, he had as much influence over me as any other man. In a good way." Johnston worked for the Secret Service for many years.

He does remember White's approach to discipline.

"We were throwing rocks one day during spring at the track; Coach found out and came over to us and said we were going to run the mile in 5:45 today and if we didn't make it we were going to do it tomorrow. That was not easy for the regular guys, maybe the track guys, but not us. I was not a track runner. I remember sprinting around that asphalt track and being exhausted at the end and diving at the finish line. I was bleeding. My brother was a track runner and he jogged across the line. Coach kind of snarled at that."

Johnston says that White was an innovator not only in his defensive and offensive philosophies but also in installing the weight program at Banks.

"When I went to Alabama, Banks had a better strength program than they did. Coach White had exercises geared specifically for football players."

Perhaps the greatest example of the benefit of Shorty White weight training is Johnny Musso, one of the best football players in Alabama high school and college history. He was a standout at Banks under White and an All-American at the University. Johnny Musso is also a member of the College Football Hall of Fame.

Musso learned the values of hard work, discipline and perseverance from both his high school and college playing days as he did from his educational experience. He has used them to create a very successful business career.

Musso remembers White as a hard driver dedicated to what he was doing and more importantly, dedicated to his players.

"As far as a high school coach, I don't think they come any better," Musso says of White. "At the time Banks High School was a wonderful place to be, particularly playing in the athletic programs, they were awesome. It was a period of time when coaches were the most influential people in the school. Coach White was in that group of people who influenced kids. He taught you values and goals, how to work together and the value of working hard. All the things football and sports can provide he did very, very well. He was also a great coach. We won a lot of games. I don't think there was a better high school coach."

Musso talks about what a focused teacher White was and what he taught his players, particularly about commitment.

"He was real determined. He demanded a great deal from you. There was an old school mentality. You look back and say that was the way things were back then. You had to give it your whole being. The expectations were very high.

"He brought a lot of energy and optimism. He surrounded himself with good people. He had a good staff. You can't judge people when you're in high school on their X's and O's knowledge, but he was very creative and cutting edge."

Musso played for White from '64 -'67. As he developed from his freshman year, Musso notes that White always took a personal interest in him as an individual and as a player. White wanted the best for his players, all of them.

"He put me on a program that he thought would make me better. He encouraged me from the end of my freshman year all the way through high school. He stayed in tune with what I was doing and he communicated the things I needed to do to make me better."

Musso talks about White from a football perspective but he learned more from White than just football. Football was very important to "Moose" and the commitment he learned from his football coach carried over into all aspects of his life. Musso has a great reflection on White's ability to motivate and his encouragement for his player to be the best he could be: "I needed to put on weight and gain strength and he would go down in the weight room and work out with me. We would kind of have a competition as to who could lift more. I was trying to move up faster than he did. Of course I was young and very determined to do that. It was a lot of fun and it made the challenge fun. He not only expected us to work but he'd get sweaty too."

"He finally got me at the end of the summer," White concedes. "I hurt my elbow lifting and it still hurts today. I knew when he beat me out on the weights that he had arrived."

Musso says there was a lot demanded of the players in the program but the times were that way. Coaches were tough then, not that they aren't now, there are plenty of solid, tough taskmasters today who have a lot of success, but the kids were very committed to what they were doing as few kids are today. There was a real dedication to the sport that is probably not as prevalent today with all the other distractions that high school kids experience. Musso still savors great rivalries in the city with Woodlawn, Ramsay, Ensley, Jones Valley, Phillips and Bessemer among others.

One of Musso's top memories was the '65 season, his sophomore year, a year in which his team finished 10-0 and was voted at the end of the season as the number one team in the state.

"There was unbelievable leadership on that team," recalls "The

Moose" who became "The Italian Stallion" at the University. "We had a good deal of talent. There were a lot of guys on the team who got scholarships and had success at higher levels too. It was about 100 percent commitment. If you didn't make the commitment, you couldn't make it. It prepared me for college football mentally. Physically you can get in shape in a matter of months but the mental part of college football I was prepared for, whereas other kids out of high school weren't."

Musso played for Bear Bryant at Alabama, quite possibly the greatest college football coach of all time. Johnny says there were a lot of similarities with White and Bryant as far as expectations went and their emphasis on commitment to what you were doing.

"They were both very demanding of their players. Quitting was a tempting option at times."

They were different in their interactions with their players though.

"Coach Bryant never got on a personal level with his players. He was very much intimidating. He used that as a motivating force. You really never felt relaxed around him enough to kid with him or put your arm around him or have any physical contact with him. Coach White was not like that. He was very approachable. He knew you on a personal level. He was not on a buddy-buddy level, that is for sure. But it was much more personal with him."

Musso says that his three-year playing experience at Banks High School along with his experience at Alabama taught him how to conduct his life when he got out into the professional world.

"It made me who I am," says Musso, happily married and living in Chicago. "It instilled in me a lot of the characteristics that have been embedded in me for all of my life. It taught me the value of commitment, perseverance, hard work, staying the course, doing the right things and riding out the highs and lows in performance levels. It taught me about winning and losing, all the things that are part of life. It taught me to stay positive, to work hard and be a contributing citizen.

"When you start out in a job you may not know much about it but you have the tools to succeed from what you learned in sports along with the schooling part of education. But I probably got a greater degree of that from my athletic experience, the things that I learned on the playing field."

Musso learned a lot about character and commitment from his days at Banks, his formative years under White.

"I remember Coach White doing it all, taping ankles, conversing with the players. It was very tense before games. He was always preparing you, talking to you, getting you focused.

"When I think of Coach White I think of him walking on his toes and bouncing around. I have a very warm image of him."

Musso of course went on to Alabama and had a stellar career for the Tide. White has often been asked what Musso meant to the team. "What would the best running back you've ever coached mean to anybody? A player like that builds everybody's confidence."

White had a profound effect on Musso and meant a lot to his personal growth and his development of character which, to this day, his peers agree is impeccable.

Larry Willingham, blessed with more speed than Johnny Musso, also reached the NFL. Larry played for White in the mid-'60s; as a defensive end and linebacker he also won a state championship on the '65 team. He went on to play at Auburn and for the St. Louis Cardinals. "I believe in winning at whatever you do and that was instilled in me at Banks," Willingham says. "I went on to play college and professional football and the lessons I learned at Banks have stuck with me furthermore in the workplace and in everything I do. I loved playing for Coach White." Willingham is now in Gulf Shores working in real estate. "I haven't seen the beach for two years."

Larry Willingham played for White at Banks from '64-'66 and as a junior was a key player on the state championship team that only allowed 36 points in 10 games. Willingham played defensive end, linebacker and wide receiver. He was a blazer on the field and he landed a scholarship to Auburn, where he went on to become an All-American cornerback his senior year. Drafted in the fourth round by the St. Louis Cardinals, Larry played a couple of years before injuries forced his retirement from the NFL. He played a couple of years for the Birmingham Americans and then Vulcans and "had a blast."

Willingham remembers that White was the ultimate teacher and disciplinarian. "Back then a coach was a coach and a player was a player and you didn't really know your coach.

"Coach White knew how to get the best out of his players and that was his strength. In high school, coaching is 65 percent of it. They scheme and design plays, they are the chess masters. The players are just pawns. Coach White and Coach Burgess taught me the fundamentals and that was what I took with me to Auburn."

Though Willingham was chosen as an All-American his senior season he believes that his junior season was his best, when he had seven interceptions. "They threw at me in the first three games of my senior year and I picked off four passes. Then they stopped throwing my way."

Willingham—a member of the Alabama Sports Hall of Fame—starred on Auburn teams that went to three bowls the three years he played. His senior year the Plainsmen played Ole Miss in the Gator Bowl. It was Pat Sullivan versus Archie Manning, and Willingham ran a punt back 54 yards for the game-winning score. His senior year in the Iron Bowl, Alabama wide receiver David Bailey and he had an epic duel. "David Bailey was one fine athlete. He caught some and I broke up some. He scored a two-point conversion on me that put them ahead. Tide quarterback, Scott Hunter, and I joke around today about the offensive interference that wasn't called on Bailey on that play."

The record shows that Sullivan took his Tigers down the field late for the game-winning touchdown.

Willingham played under Bill Oliver, a tremendous teacher just hitting his stride in the coaching business. There were two other All-SEC players in the defensive backfield and one of them was an All-American, Willingham's junior year.

Willingham says the '65 team at Banks was a great group of guys, highly athletic and talented. They never caused trouble and if they did White would bring the hammer down. "We would be considered boring today with all these guys do."

White's Larry W. played at St. Louis with Larry Wilson, an All-Pro for many years who was selected for the Pro Football Hall of Fame. "I learned from some of the best. I feel very fortunate."

Today Larry is in real estate where he started his career in Birmingham after hanging up his helmet. He worked in real estate in the Magic City until interest rates went up to 20 percent, then he went to Rust International, where he worked for some time before getting into industrial sales for 15 years. He got an offer from his brother to buy part of a house in Gulf Shores three and a half years ago and lives in Gulf Shores today. He is hard at work in the real estate business again.

"What I learned from football is that you work hard and there is a reward at the end of the trail. There is no substitute for it. Coach White taught me that, as did my other coaches through the years. It's tough sometimes when you're on the Gulf of Mexico. I've got a 20-foot boat that I haven't seen this year. Gulf Shores is a small town and everybody knows everybody. The track facility down here is tremendous. It's a great place to live."

Willingham played for the legendary Shug Jordan at Auburn. He says the experience was memorable.

"He was a manager of people. When he yelled at us or his assistant coaches, we would listen. We knew who was boss."

Larry took great pleasure in seeing White this past spring. Larry went to the state track meet in Gulf Shores and was thinking about White on the way to the meet. When he got to the meet he saw a smaller man with a brimmed hat and a big smile on his face. It was White coming to see his grandson Riley compete.

"We talked and I said that I was in this same meet 40 years ago. We talked about things. He had run me in the city meet before that and I had already run my fourth event, I was dog tired and he wanted me to run the mile relay. I had never run a quarter before but he walked me down the field and said I could do it. Well I got lapped in the race and just basically fell out after I ran. He told me after that that he'd guessed I couldn't run the quarter. My mother would have killed him that day had she known he did that."

But Willingham thinks often about his former coach today. "I love him to death."

Willingham says that while high school was 65 percent coaching, college was still 60 percent though there was a lot more thinking on the players' part. In the pros it's all about players, with coaches being kind of the taskmasters.

"In the pros, we would be in a meeting and a coach would go over the scheme and three or four players would say we can't do that with our physical limitations. There was a ton of input from the players and I called a lot of the coverages and change of coverages. We had to think a lot out there. We were audibilizing just like the quarterback does. I was young and not married but didn't like St. Louis that much. Most of the guys were married and it was a job for them. I had a ball playing though, particularly when I came to Birmingham and played."

CHAPTER 10
Setting the Stage (1966-1971)

White looks back on the special '65 season with tremendous satisfaction. It was a year in which he came into his own as a coach and coached players who believed in him and his coaches and worked hard, both on and off the field, succeeding at Banks and then succeeding in life. It was a highly gratifying year for a coach coming into his own and laying the foundation for unprecedented success in Alabama high school football.

White reflects on the magical 10-0 season that led to a state championship as voted on by the sportswriters throughout the state. There was no playoff in '65. The playoff format began the next year.

"When it's the first time it makes it that much more special. What it did for me is it gave me confidence in my ability to coach. We hadn't had a lot of success before that. We knew that now that we had the athletes we had a chance to win. I had good assistant coaches. I couldn't keep 'em long enough. A coach said to me one time that every time you lose a coach off your staff it costs you at least one ball game. I'd lose two at a time. But if my coaches weren't ambitious, I didn't want them on my staff."

White's players were excited after the title win, shaking hands and patting each other on the back for a job well done. They were not a showy bunch, handling winning with dignity and class but they were excited about the undefeated season, no doubt about it. They had put so much work into it that there was a lot of elation after the season concluded with a perfect ending.

"There was not a playoff then," White says. "I wish there had been. But we deserved it. We were the only team in our class to go undefeated."

Banks scored 203 points and gave up only 36 in '65. They had six shutouts.

"What made that team so good was our defense. We were hard to score on. Without question, those guys loved to play defense and we had the personnel to play it."

Beating the likes of Woodlawn, Ramsay twice, coached by Mutt Reynolds, one of the better coaches in the state, Jones Valley and Bessemer among others was no easy task. As a matter of fact it was very difficult. City football was probably the best in the state at the time.

"There were some good coaches in the city," White recalls. "I thought we didn't do right to leave Sylacauga to come here."

But it turned out to be a great move for a man who loved his job and loved Banks High School.

"I couldn't have asked for a better environment," he says. "Everybody pulled together. We cried together, we laughed together, we lost together and we won together. We had some pretty little girls too. Those boys had it made. If you couldn't find somebody, something was wrong with you."

White also says that his job was something he woke up and was eager to get to.

"I couldn't wait to get down there to that school. No matter what kind of money you're making, if you look forward to getting to the workplace whether you're a businessman, mechanic or bus driver, you have the best in life."

White had eight seniors earn college football scholarships off the team: Sam Chambliss, Merrill Mann, Johnny Johnston, Allan Girardeau, Rhett Wood, Billy Strickland, Ronnie Massie and Jeff Masters.

The '66 season was good, not great for White though his team did win the city sportsmanship award, which was important to him. White made his acceptance speech and talked about playing with integrity and character and how it prepared you for life, whether you were a football player or a regular student. He had a tragedy on his football team in the spring before the '66 season. Banks was conducting a bull-in-the-ring drill; White and the coaches had preached to the players to keep their head down when they hit an opposing player. In the drill, one player would get in the middle of the ring and the other players would have numbers. When their number was called, they would hit the player in the middle of the ring. Randy Baker had his head up when he took a hit from a 140-pound freshman. Baker was a freshman as well. He had a bruise on his chin and the hit broke his neck. He died from the hit.

"We really had preached to the players to keep their chin down when they hit each other," White says. "I thought my assistant coach who was conducting the drill would never get over it. The amazing thing about it was that Randy had written his dad a note weeks before that he would die that year. It was a terrible situation." Three other Banks students, non-athletes, died that year: Marvin Waites, Beth Corley and Larry Williams.

The '66 team went 7-2 and five players earned college scholarships: Rusty Morrow (Arkansas), Mike Pitts (The Citadel), Kirk Stallings (Mississippi State), Ken Wahlers (Auburn), and Larry Willingham who became an All-American at Auburn and a standout in the NFL for the St. Louis Cardinals.

White guided his '67 team to a 7-3 record. Bob Phares and Johnny "The Moose" Musso were stallions at running back for White. White lost to Ensley 30-14 in the regular season, probably the most points a Banks defense had ever given up, but he got a shot at redemption in the Clinic game that the Jets took advantage of it. Moose ran for 194 yards, Phares 123 and sophomore quarterback Gary Rutledge threw for 93 yards and scored a touchdown as Banks whipped Ensley 28-7. White had put in a new offense going to split backs instead of a power I backfield. It worked to perfection. "We pulled both guards, blocked down and smashed 'em in the mouth," he says. "We ran the Green Bay sweep like Lombardi was running."

White's coaches that year were Ronnie Baynes, a legend in high school baseball coaching who won five state championships in baseball at Tallassee and is now head of the NFL referees, Bobby Lott, Howard Kitchens and Jim Currier.

"Jim and Ronnie were very good coaches. Ronnie called the defensive signals during the games."

The parents had earlier acquired a jet that the school brought from the airport. It became a symbol. "Woodlawn would try to come over and mess with it and paint it. I put some boys out there and the hooligans didn't come back."

On the way back from the airport, White and the men encountered a man driving fast on the road. "He stopped the car and said, 'My wife is never going to believe this.' The police came over to talk to the man. He was drunk. They hauled him away."

Phil Cochran went to Auburn but ended up playing at Troy State. "He could play anywhere on the field." One of White's favorites was John Howard, who played tight end for him and went on to play at Trinity in Texas. "I was on the staff in the high school All-Star game and we needed a tight end. I told the coaches I had a guy who I knew would be a good player. I called him and told him to come down and play for us. John said,

'When Coach?' I said 'Right now.' He played in the game and did a great job. It proved to me he could have played in the SEC."

White also had an emerging young star quarterback in sophomore Gary Rutledge.

"He had a great head on his shoulders," White says. "He led us to a 4-1 end of '67. Everybody respected him. He was a leader on and off the field. He didn't demand it, he was just such a good person."

White's '68 team went 7-2-1. In the first game at Robert E. Lee in Montgomery, the Banks fans had to sit on the Lee side because of renovations to the stadium. The Lee fans were all making bets and a Jets' parent made one bet that the Banks first touchdown would be called back because of a penalty.

Sure enough Bob Phares raced for a 60-yard score and it was called back. The Banks parent collected $25. Banks won the game though 21-20. They went on to beat Minor, who White says, was a good football team, 27-0, defeated Woodlawn 28-7, Phillips 46-0 and Ramsay 10-7.

"We went up to Coffee and Herbie Kirby of *The Birmingham News* picked us to win by 66," White says. "I knew that was going to be a problem. My players were acting up all week. They were fat-headed."

Banks lost to Coffee 17-7.

"I was so mad I called him up after the game and told him he cost us the ball game," White says. "But then I figured maybe it'll help us grow up. I told my coaches after the game we'll see what this team is made of."

Banks went on to beat West End 26-13, tie Ensley 7-7, beat Jones Valley 13-0 and lose to Ramsay 8-6.

In '69, the Jets posted an 8-2 mark. They blasted Parker 55-6 in the first integrated football game in Alabama.

Banks started out 4-0 but then lost to Berry and legendary coach Bob Finley whom White had the utmost respect for. Berry defeated Banks 9-7 in a hard-fought, physical game. Gary Rutledge was the punter for Banks and was in the end zone in the key play of the game. He was in the very back of the end zone and White says he hadn't noticed it, but Rutledge took one step back with his right foot and stepped on the back line before taking two steps and punting the ball. Banks was called for a safety and lost the game.

"I learned a coaching lesson from that game," White ruefully recalls. "It never happened again."

Banks went through the rest of the season without a defeat before losing to Woodlawn and Coach Bill Burgess 28-20 to end the season.

"Woodlawn had played four games in a span of two weeks and

they finished the season undefeated," White says. "Coach Burgess was a good football coach. They lost in the first round of the playoffs. I think they were beaten down from playing so many games in a short period of time."

After the '69 season, White was back at work getting his team ready for a run in the 70's for what would become the glory years for Banks High School.

The '70 and '71 seasons were not White's best years because the talent level was not where it had been in the mid- and late-60's. He still had good players but maybe not enough of them. But his younger teams, the freshman team and the B team, won city championships and were setting the table for great things to happen for Banks High School.

The 1970 team, led by Rick Neel at tailback, finished the season around .500 and the 1971 team posted a 5-5 mark. The most memorable moment for White in 1971 was the Mountain Brook game—his team was losing 15-13 late in the game when White called a fake field goal on fourth down. White's holder took the snap from center, stood up and completed a pass for a first down deep in Mountain Brook territory. The official ruled that the holder was on his knee when he received the snap and was thus considered down. White couldn't believe it and vehemently protested the call. The call stood and Mountain Brook won the game 15-13.

Later White's team lost to Jones Valley 27-13. White thinks Jones Valley sent five players to SEC schools that year. Banks then defeated Ramsay 35-8 and Phillips 15-14. In the Phillips game, Banks trailed 14-0 when White inserted freshman quarterback Jeff Rutledge. Rutledge led the Banks comeback. That was the start of something special for the program with a quarterback who would lead White's teams to greater heights and three special seasons. Banks then lost to Huffman 21-0. White notes this Huffman team was the best they ever had. Woodlawn under new coach Tandy Geralds defeated Banks 21-18. White learned that the Huffman players said they were not going to lose to a freshman quarterback.

White knew he had a stellar group coming up the pipeline. "Our B team and freshman teams in '69 and '70 were winners," he says. "We had some good young ones coming."

White always coached three sports. In the early 70's he was coaching football, wrestling and track. "You got paid for each of the sports you coached," he says. "I would have coached the marbles team for $100."

They were tough times financially.

"All I did was turn the check over to June," White says. "She did wonders with so little." But White was extremely successful and you can't measure that kind of success in dollars and cents. It's an invaluable contribution to society.

Jimmy Carroll and Bobby Johns were his assistants. Mike Dutton also assisted and was coach of the city champion freshman team.

White had some players. David Cutcliffe became a highly successful assistant coach at Tennessee, where he tutored Peyton Manning, and then coached his brother Eli at Ole Miss where Cutcliffe was the head coach. Cutcliffe is now back at Tennessee as the Volunteers' offensive coordinator. Tim Nichols was a co-captain and an intelligent young man, according to White. He played at 195 pounds, big in 1970. Dennis Gallups was a cornerback who was "quick as a hiccup". Gallups, White says, gave 100 percent effort all the time. His father was a highway patrolman:

"I was driving down I-59 coming back from a recruiting trip in Gadsden for Alabama when this highway patrolman pulls me over for speeding. It was Dennis's dad. He said he'd let me go but that it better not happen again."

Steve Randal was a defensive back who had real good speed. Rodney Roundtree played for White. He once said to White, "My mother knows you, she went to school with you."

Tommy Smith was a smart kid who played free safety for Shorty. "He was not big but could run pretty good. He did super in business," White says. Alan Atkins was a tight end who gave a lot of effort, same with Kim Dale and Randy Durbin who was good-sized. Other key players were Kenny Brown, Bill Burwell, Terry Coggins, Benny Gray and Jimmy Gustin, Roger Harper, Jimmy Johnson, Larry Riddle, Sammy Webb and Phil Wentzell. All of these players gave great effort, according to White. That was a mark of all his teams.

Before the 1970 season, tragedy struck. One of his best players, Tony Wagnon, who White says, was always waiting for him at the weight shack after summer school was out, so he could get started "pumping steel" and get his running in, was driving his Volkswagen up a hill, taking his girlfriend home from a date. An intoxicated woman crashed head on into Wagnon. Wagnon's head struck the steering wheel and he passed out.

Wagnon's girlfriend was thrown through the windshield. The car went up in flames. A man heard the crash and came out to see what happened. He saw the car in flames with Wagnon in it. He went back to his house and got a blanket. He could not get the door open, but Wagnon regained consciousness and slammed the door open with his forearm.

"That's how strong he was," White says. "He was going to be another Musso for us."

Wagnon died on the way to the hospital. "It was so depressing," White laments. "All you could do with his family is offer your sympathy. He was going to Alabama (on a football scholarship) and he knew it. It was like losing a son. I had been with him three going on four years. It was like family.

"You don't start thinking about the game of football, you think about life. There is no comparison. We lost three kids when I was coaching. We lost two players in freshman on freshman drills. I would have given up coaching to save those three lives. We had to go back on the field after Tony Wagnon's death and Max Booker and Randy Baker died in football drills. The kids were scared, you're scared. I can still see them today. Those kids were part of our football program and were just as valuable as anybody who played. They were good Christian kids. I know where they are today." We had very few discipline problems because of the way we handled kids who broke the rules. It cost us in the won-loss column."

White was demanding discipline in some very difficult times to do so. These were the early 70's and the anti-war, hippie era was in full swing. It was the beginning stages of drugs, though there were very few cases at Banks and no athletes were involved.

"They were trying times. We had problems in the school and we had catastrophes. I think I got out of it at the right time."

But it was still a great place to be. White attributes some of his success to the parents who supported him 100 percent. They were very active parents, a huge help to the program. One of White's favorites was Phil Neel, who was Rick Neel's dad. Rick's brother Mike was on White's teams in the 60's and became a captain at Auburn. Shug Jordan called Mike Neel one of his favorite players.

Phil is an artist who put together pictures of the '65, '72, '73 and '74 teams with the players on the team, the coaches, the scores of the games and the final records. He also painted a caricature of each player in the picture. It's first-rate memorabilia of ultra-successful seasons.

One game Phil didn't think Rick, his son, was giving maximum effort.

"I was walking off the field at halftime and I was a little late getting off because I think a reporter had been asking me questions," White says. "I saw Phil getting in his son's face about not giving enough effort on the field. Rick's dad was chewing him out. Wow! He followed him to the locker room and then said to me that his son was not giving any effort. I just said to Rick, you know you need to give it 100 percent now or it's not going to be fun for you after the game. Rick always gave 100 percent effort and after his father gave him that little talk at halftime, he sure gave it everything he had. Rick was a dominant player in the second half and Banks won the game."

When the playoffs were instituted in 1967 a team would have to play 13 games to win a state championship. White believes that's the number of games that ought to be played today.

"I think that is enough. You look at the college game and they don't play that many because of academics and injuries. I think the city and county ought to play a Classic game with the winner of the city schools playing the winner of the county schools and sure, have a 10-game regular season. But then finish up with just 13 games."

Shorty has a point. Injuries pile up playing 15 games and school becomes an afterthought when teams are in the playoffs. A 13-game season is plenty.

White finished the '71 season with a .500 mark. But in that season he discovered one special player. During the Phillips game with Banks losing 14-0, White inserted freshman Jeff Rutledge at quarterback. White told Rutledge to go into the huddle and say something positive to his teammates to give them confidence in him, something they could build on. Rutledge uttered something in the huddle that energized his teammates, and he led them to a 15-14 victory. After the game White asked a couple of the seniors what Rutledge had said. They told him he said, "I have confidence in you and I have confidence in myself. Now let's start moving the football." A .500 record was something Banks and White would never get used to and to White it was truly unacceptable. That wasn't going to be the case any longer as there were some superstars in the pipeline for the Jets and some special seasons in store.

Yes, there were some special individuals coming up in those years. For example, Bill Jones, a wrestler for White from his ninth grade through twelfth grade years: Jones was an admitted small guy—he weighed 80 pounds in ninth grade in '64.

"Coach White was a good friend of my father, Hooley Jones. They played football at Phillips in '49 and '50 on some good teams. My Dad was a running back, as was White. Coach came over to me in the lunchroom my freshman year and I was scared to death. He was already a legendary coach and you could hear a pin drop. When he came over to me everybody was silent. He had immediate success on the football field after he started in '61. He asked me if I'd thought about wrestling. I decided to do it. He told me he needed somebody to wrestle at 95 pounds. I ended up wrestling for him for four years and I lettered as a freshman. I wasn't that great, but I got a letter all four years."

Jones remembers White as maybe not the most technically adept wrestling coach—football was his passion—but he was so competitive and really liked his football players to wrestle to have an off-season regimen. White would have his football players wrestle at the higher weight classes.

"It gave me confidence. He was a real taskmaster. He was so organized. Practice started at 2 p.m. boom and every 15-minute period was so organized."

Jones also played baseball. His senior year he was president of the student body. His junior year he talked to the college counselor at Banks, Bill Jenkins, whom Jones calls a great guy. Jenkins asked him where he wanted to go to college. Jones made excellent grades and told Jenkins he thought he wanted to go to Alabama. Jenkins told him to look around. Jones applied to Brown, Vanderbilt, SMU and Virginia. Jones got a full four-year scholarship to Virginia, a DuPont scholarship named after the chemical company.

"I couldn't have afforded to go there if it weren't for the scholarship," reflects today's President of O'Neal Steel, one of the premier steel companies in the country. Jones has been president since 2000.

He and Johnny Musso were in the same class and Musso was president of the student body in the spring after Jones had been in the fall. You could only serve as president one semester and Jones says that Musso "could do it all." They talk every month today.

Jones remembers White as dedicated to his job and his athletes.

"If you met him at least halfway and did what he told you to do, you would most likely win and whether you won or lost, he respected you for your hard work. He was just driven to make you better. He was really ahead of his time in so many areas. I know a lot of people have said that. He absolutely loved and cherished his football team and his players."

Another one of those transition players became quite a coaching legend in the college game. Master motivator and offensive mind, David Cutcliffe put the University of Tennessee back on the map amongst the powers of college football. Cutcliffe is known for his discipline and his ability to dissect a defense and maximize his offensive players' skills, particularly those of his quarterback.

He is also a fine person who believes in integrity and discipline in all of his players' lives. That is part of his winning program.

He resurrected a Tennessee offense that became one of the best in the country. Peyton Manning, who played under Cutcliffe at Tennessee, told Erik Ainge, Tennessee's starter in 2006, to shut up and listen to everything that Cutcliffe would tell him. That formula worked well for Ainge as he became the best quarterback in the conference.

Cutcliffe got his inspiration to coach under White at Banks. Cutcliffe played both offense and defense for White in the late 60's. He remembers Shorty being tough, hard-nosed and demanding.

"The first thing that comes to mind is that we were all scared to death of him. He was a strict disciplinarian and he was intense all the time. He was in control. I learned a lot about coaching from him."

David also remembers how meticulous White was in everything he did, from coaching the offense and defense to prepping all aspects of his football program.

"Whether it was the equipment room or the locker room or his office, everything was neatly placed. We were polished."

White was a master of teaching fundamental football, in Cutcliffe's view.

"Sometimes we'd practice without a football. He made you understand the fundamentals of the game. It was a great experience."

Cutcliffe says that White was also focused on developing character in his players off the field. He emphasized personal conduct.

"All of us who played for Coach White became better people. He talked about his expectations for us off the field, how we conducted ourselves in the hallways in school. He had zero tolerance for alcohol. We need more of that today in school with kids. He was a strict disciplinarian."

Cutcliffe remembers two things that stick out in his mind from his playing days for White.

"He's the greatest punter of all time as far as I'm concerned. He would stand on the porch on our gym where there was a high railing in front and a low ceiling and he would punt the football across the street to the practice field. The stock in Honda and Yamaha went down because he'd kick you off the team if you had a motorcycle.

"He also hated golfers. He thought everybody should be working all the time. I can remember riding with him in the car and him hollering at golfers."

There was also the softer side of White that he rarely showed to his football team but that was present. When his players had personal difficulties White was always there for them.

"I lost my father when I was in high school and Coach was very instrumental to me, just being a father figure. He gave me the discipline and the structure that I needed. I took a lot longer look at him than a lot of other guys. I remember that look in his eyes when he was concerned about you. He grew up pretty tough and he had that side to him. He never let his guard down but you knew he was there when you were going through tough times."

Cutcliffe knew his coach cared a lot about him. This man who could instill great fear in his players was mostly concerned with his players' well-being.

White was also in tremendous physical shape according to David, and had tons of energy.

"I remember him going 900 miles an hour. For his age he was incredibly fit. I remember his energy being second to none."

White also took pride in his players being the best students they could be.

"He was all about academic integrity. He was as good an educator as you could find."

Cutcliffe has had his own success on the football field and talking to him you can tell there is a lot of personal integrity in the man. He has tutored Peyton and Eli Manning. Peyton was obviously extremely successful on the football field as he was the top college quarterback at Tennessee and is the best quarterback in the NFL today. Cutcliffe coached Eli Manning at Ole Miss and led the Rebels to a 10-3 record in 2003. He was unjustly fired in 2004 after a 4-7 rebuilding season. He has proven he is back and can coach offensive football with the best in the business. David deserves another shot at a college head coaching job. One hopes he will get it.

Cutcliffe is quick to say it would be a travesty if White were not inducted into the Alabama Sports Hall of Fame, with all he has accomplished both at Banks and at the University of Alabama, where he coached running backs from 1975-81.

"He was unbelievably successful. I'd like to see that documented in the Hall of Fame. He was great on the high school level for a long time and on the college level as well.

"He was ahead of his time as a coach. He had the Veer option in before a lot of coaches did. He could read the triple option and had a nice drop back passing game. He had a great feel for the game. He got the triple option from Bill Yeomen at Houston and got a lot of the Veer principles and brought them back to Alabama. He developed great running backs and great quarterbacks. There was talent all over the place at Banks."

Cutcliffe learned how to lead young men in the right path, to teach principles and fundamentals of the game and to be the best football coach he could be—which is pretty doggone good—from White. He has unparalleled respect for a man who had a major impact on his life.

"I respect and admire Coach White immensely."

So does an undersized legend at Banks High School, Gary Rutledge, who credits Coach White with instilling in him the discipline it took to succeed on the football field, and credits him with teaching him the tools to become a very good college quarterback at the University of Alabama.

Rutledge was a starter for White in '67, '68 and '69 running the triple-option, Veer offense that White perfected at Banks. Rutledge was an outstanding runner and an effective passer. He recalls White as an intense football coach who was all about maximizing his talent and preparing his teams to the utmost for victory on Friday nights.

"He made me a better athlete, a better football player," Rutledge says. "I remember him as just being tough, tough on all the players who played for him. He was a disciplinarian kind of guy. He was always pushing me, pushing me, pushing me. You didn't know whether he liked you or not, because he was always focused on winning football games."

White's strict code of discipline carried over into all aspects of his football program, particularly the way he expected his players to appear and act.

"He wouldn't put up with any nonsense from any of the players," said Gary, whose younger brother Jeff played for White from '71-'74. "He didn't like long hair, he didn't like you having girlfriends. He was old-fashioned like that. I used to come home and tell my dad that Coach White doesn't like me, all he does is yell at me. My dad would always say—because he was an athlete—if he didn't like you he wouldn't speak to you and be on you all the time. He likes you, he cares and he wants you to do better. He tried to tell me that Coach White liked me. I sure couldn't see it. He never got close to his players. Winning football games was all he cared about at Banks High School."

Of course White cared about his players as people and today he talks about his former players with much affection. When White talks about his players he says they were a "special" group. Gary Rutledge was one of his favorites.

Rutledge says that White was a master at preparing his teams for games. He put his players through military-style practices that stressed fundamentals, preparation for the opponent and intense conditioning.

"Practice was tough every day mentally and physically. He pushed you. But he prepared our football teams extremely well. He would give us great motivational talks and have us ready to play the game. He knew what the other team was going to run offensively and defensively." Rutledge says the teams he played on only lost one or two games a year but in those times only four teams would play in the playoffs in each class. There were four classes in Alabama at the time. This changed to six classes in the '80s. "We had a chance to go my senior year but we lost to Berry. Back then we had Woodlawn and Berry, teams like that who were pretty good every year.

Rutledge got a chance to play his sophomore year and says he spent the time handing off to Johnny Musso, which he enjoyed, as Musso churned up the yards.

"Johnny gave me the name "Rooster" because my hair was red like the top of the head of a rooster."

Rutledge says White's coaching at Banks put Gary way ahead of the other high school players in his recruiting class at Alabama. "I found out that I had been very well coached when I started at Alabama. They started running the Wishbone when I was there and that was right up my alley."

The Wishbone used the same principles as the triple-option, Veer offense White ran at Banks though Rutledge's dad Jack was always yelling from the stands, "Throw the ball Shorty!" Rutledge started for Alabama as a junior and then led the team to a highly successful season in '73, his senior year, when they played for the national championship against Notre Dame in the 1974 Sugar Bowl. Notre Dame won a classic over the Tide 24-23 to capture the title. Rutledge was a great running and passing quarterback out of the Wishbone.

"I owe Coach White a lot for my success at Alabama," Rutledge says. "He was big on character and family. He was about being a leader. He believed that an athlete should be an example to the rest of the school. If you played football for Banks you represented him. He wanted you to toe the mark and be the kind of person you were supposed to be. My dad really liked him. My dad would be hollering at him to throw the ball when I was quarterback but we won and that was the bottom line."

Rutledge saw many similarities between White and Coach Bryant, his college coach.

"Both were well organized and both had great assistant coaches. I knew going in what to expect from the other team. They both believed in discipline and preparedness. They demanded excellence and perfection. Winning was the only object. To practice was to win and they both got the most out of their players. Coach White motivated us but he motivated us by fear. He would chew you out in a heartbeat no matter if you were a starter or a third-stringer. He got the most out of you, which Coach Bryant did too."

Rutledge remembers that White would push him and his

teammates to the limit and drive them to try to achieve perfection, a characteristic of many successful coaches.

"You didn't know you had it in you until he pushed you. I knew to be the starting quarterback I'd better play well or I'd be benched."

Gary says that he and Jeff would not talk much when he was at Alabama and Jeff was at Banks. Gary was busy getting ready for college football games during the week. He does say Jeff was heavily recruited by LSU and believes that Jeff might have excelled even more in Baton Rouge and would have been a higher draft pick in the NFL because LSU threw the ball more than Alabama. But Rutledge also notes his younger brother felt it was better to go to the in-state university, as it would help him down the road in whatever field he pursued. Jeff did play in the NFL for 14 years.

"I played at only 6-1, 180 pounds," Gary remembers. "I was too small for the pros. I was a good runner but my arm was not very strong. But when you see guys like Fran Tarkenton you think there was a chance."

Rutledge says that White had a similar approach to what Hoover coach Rush Propst employs today.

"I think we could have hung with them if we played, if not beat them. We had good athletes. Jeff's group probably had better athletes than we did, but we had some good offensive linemen and backs. We were not as big as Hoover but I think we would have done really well, especially having Coach White as our coach. Coach White was somewhat like Rush Propst but he didn't use the curse words. Coach was intense. If you didn't give 100 percent he'd find somebody else real quick."

And Gary Rutledge is convinced White would succeed today.

"Without a doubt. He hasn't aged a bit as far as I'm concerned. He could win with kids today. Yeah, they're a little different but I don't think Coach White has changed a bit with his attitude and hard work. He could get his kids ready, I guarantee you."

A man who could help him do that is Jim Currier, one of White's top assistants in the late 60's and early 70's. He went on to become a fine head football coach in the Alabama high school ranks at Springville, Jacksonville and Pinson Valley. Currier won county championships at each stop and developed top state wrestling programs at each school. He coached Alabama All-American Warren Lyles and standouts Anthony Smiley and Dwayne Vaughn, a two-time state decathlon winner.

Currier coached multiple positions at Banks for White; Shorty told him that he was going to be a successful head coach one day. He groomed him for that job as White did with many of his assistants who went on to become very successful head coaches.

Currier coached B team football, track and basketball at Jones Valley and enjoyed success against Banks.

White asked Jim to come to Banks, and Currier accepted the offer.

Currier, who still considers White his best friend and talks to him today, calls White "a man of principle and integrity."

Currier remembers a good example of White's integrity.

"We were in a track meet with Woodlawn and Banks when I was the track coach at Jones Valley and we thought that was a big deal because Banks and Woodlawn were big programs in the state. Banks beat us in the mile relay to win the meet, but Shorty called me after the meet and told me that actually we had won, because he had mistakenly entered Larry Willingham, his runner, in an event that was Willingham's sixth event, which was not allowed. I didn't even realize it. The next day it was in the paper that we had won and Shorty didn't even mention anything about Willingham. He did not have to do that. That was just the way he was."

Currier admired White for his convictions. He tried to emulate him.

"We were not politicians. If you wanted to know an opinion and it differed from yours, you'd better not ask. He would tell you what he thought, no matter what."

And Jim says that White certainly knew the game of football and how to teach it to his teams.

"He had an outstanding football mind. He was as good of a coach as I've been around. He was sharp. If there was something we needed to learn we would go somewhere like Texas, Tennessee or the University of Georgia and talk to their coaches. We gained a lot of knowledge and blended it in to what we were doing." Currier is presently helping out the program at Hayes High School in Birmingham, using the same weight program that White employed at Banks. He says the kids are "super" and sees no difference between the kids today and the kids he worked with at Banks. He believes Hayes football is getting better.

Currier says the amazing thing about White and his coaching staff's achievements was that they were done with kids strictly from the Banks High School area.

"We did it with kids zoned for Banks. We worked with the athletes we had."

Currier says that the Banks weight program White used that led to the state championship teams in '65, '72 and '73 was patterned after the Georgia program under Vince Dooley. Dooley patterned his program after the Eastern Bloc nations' program in Europe after he went over to counsel them one summer. It was a program the East Germans and others had used to win multiple Olympic gold medals.

Currier knows that White was strictly business on the football field.

"When it was time to work, we worked, when it was time to get serious, we got serious. And when it was time to laugh, we laughed. We decided that nobody was going to outwork us. The only way they were going to beat us was to outsmart us."

And that didn't happen very often either.

Currier observed a humility about Shorty.

"He never got caught up in himself. He always lived by doing what was right and letting the chips fall where they may."

And Currier says it helped having the quality of kids that he and White coached at Banks.

"The kids at Banks were first-class young men. They were winners not just on the football field but off the field in the classroom. They made our job easier."

Currier insists that White was the consummate coach who would have excelled in college as a head coach.

"There's not a nicer person. He did a good job at Alabama and would have done a good job as a college head coach. He had a chance to get the Jacksonville State job but Charley Pell got it. He was organized and meticulous."

And so is Mike Dutton, who has been coaching and teaching for 39 years in Alabama, concentrating his efforts in the Birmingham area. He calls Shorty White the best high school football coach, along with Bob Finley, that he's ever seen.

Dutton played B team basketball for White at Banks when he was a sophomore and White led the team to a 22-2 record and a city championship. While football was his passion, White was a dedicated and driven basketball coach as well.

Finley and White were colleagues and friends as well as football rivals in the 60's and 70's and Dutton says they were the best he's ever seen.

"They were the two greatest. They were two great men and they were big-time coaches. Coach Finley, who coached at Berry High School—now Hoover, was about as classy a person as ever walked the sideline. He and Coach White were the best."

Dutton, 62 in April 2008, is a superb basketball coach. He coached at Pinson Valley 17 years and led his teams to the state playoffs five times. His 2001-02 team won 28 games and made the Sweet 16 where they lost to an ultra-talented John Carroll team that featured Ronald Steele and Emmet Thomas. Steele has been the starting point guard at Alabama and a potential All-American and Thomas was a standout for the University.

Dutton is now the head basketball coach at Mortimer Jordan High School in Morris where he has lived for the past seven years. He wanted the challenge of building a program. He is huge on fundamentals and spends many of his practices working on dribbling, passing, defensive fundamentals, shooting—both jumpers and free throws. He learned the value of fundamentals from playing and coaching at Banks under White and basketball coach Albert Morton. Banks won the city championship— over a highly competitive group of schools—his senior year. Two of the players off that team went on to play at Birmingham-Southern.

White hired Dutton to coach ninth grade football and basketball when Dutton was 24 years old.

"He was a strict disciplinarian as my coach, I was scared to death of him. He was strictly business but always fair. He was a hard worker— golly, he worked us. It was a great, great experience playing for Coach White and Coach Morton, and Dewell Crumpton was also a wonderful guy. They had such an impact on our lives. As a 17-year-old you don't appreciate it as much but as a 61-year-old I sure do appreciate what those men did for me."

Dutton declares that White just took over from Jimmy Tarrant and built the best high school football program in the South.

"The thing that impressed me is that he could take average players and make them winners. He had guards who weighed 160-170 pounds and had them playing like they were 215-220. Coach White got that much out of his players. He had a knack for picking the average guys who had heart and competitiveness and would really battle for you, and he'd win a lot of games with them. Then he could take a great player like Jeff Rutledge or Johnny Musso and make him even better."

To Dutton, what separated White from other coaches—and there were many good ones in town and throughout the state—was his passion for his work.

"He was the hardest worker that I've ever been around. He was the most dedicated as far as trying to improve his knowledge of the game. He'd go to Houston to learn their offense and he was really innovative with weight training. Banks was way ahead of everybody else."

Mike adds that White's attention to detail also made him great.

"It started in the equipment room. The jerseys were folded, the helmets were in place and everybody's shoes were shined, even the coaches'. It was like being in Marine Corps basic training.

"When we used to go to Legion Field for games he made us polish our coaching shoes and he would inspect them. We were representing Banks High School and the community and we were not going to Legion Field with our shoes dirty. He'd look at the shoes and say 'OK you're ready.'

"And practices were timed right down to the minute. It was go, go, go, go, go. I learned so much about football in my four years there ('69-'73)." Dutton sees similarities between White and Rush Propst. Dutton points to their love of the game and enthusiasm and dedication to their jobs. White and Propst both have many players who have played Division One football. I asked Dutton if the Banks teams of '72, '73 or '74 were to play the Hoover teams of today, what would happen?

"You can't argue with Rush Propst's record. They probably have more depth than we had. But I think we could have beaten 'em. That's an old Banks boy talking. We had some great quarterbacks in Jeff Rutledge and Gary Rutledge. I tell you what, Coach White would have spent 24 hours a day preparing for 'em. He would have been super-motivated for that. We had guys like Jerry McDonald and Jerry Murphree who got college football scholarships. There were so many Division One players off those '72, '73 and '74 teams. We could definitely match up with them."

Dutton believes there is no doubt White should be in the Alabama High School Hall of Fame.

"I sure would love for him to be in. He had such an impact in the 60's and 70's and as a college football coach at Alabama."

Dutton says that football in the city was so good in the 60's and 70's with huge rivalries, none bigger than Banks and Woodlawn. Huffman grew to be a big rivalry in the early 70's and there was Ensley, Jones Valley, West End and Ramsay.

"These were terrific rivalries. Woodlawn and us was something special. You had to be ready to play every night out. Banks was the king so we got everybody's best ball game.

"When we played Woodlawn in '74 at Legion Field—I had never been to a high school game like that. There were two All-Americans in Jeff Rutledge and Tony Nathan. Schools that were four or five miles apart at most and the anticipation was unbelievable. It was quite a night."

Mike Dutton believes that Shorty White could succeed in any era.

"He could coach anywhere and succeed. He was so demanding but I think Rush Propst is demanding. Parents today may not be as supportive as they were at Banks. The parents were totally supportive. He'd be a terrific coach in any era."

Dutton calls White's character "impeccable, flawless. He was in a fish bowl at Banks and he was a great family man and a strong moral person. I can't say enough about him in that regard. In my opinion he is the best that Alabama has seen. He and Coach Finley; there's not much better than that.

"And he always makes the effort to get back to any gatherings or funerals for one of his former coaches or players. He was the toughest coach I've ever known but he has a big, big heart."

One of White's tougher disciples, Ronnie Baynes is a legend in athletics in Alabama. He was a fine football coach at Selma High School and at Tallassee High School, where he coached many successful teams, but he made his real mark on the baseball field leading Tallassee High School to five state championships in Class 4A in the mid- and late-80's and the early 90's. He finished up his coaching in Alexander City where he took his team to the Junior College World Series his last season as head baseball coach.

Baynes has also had a fine career as a football referee. He was a Southeastern Conference referee for thirteen years, then went on to the NFL where he called games for fourteen seasons. He was a part of the staff that called the 1995 Super Bowl between San Francisco and Denver. For the past six years he has been supervisor of referees for the NFL, reviewing games and critiquing officials. He spends four days a week in New York, then travels home to Birmingham to be with his wife during the NFL season. He has retired from coaching.

The Talledega native also was an outstanding athlete. He was an outstanding football player at Auburn and a baseball player as well. Ronnie was drafted by the Dallas Cowboys, but a knee injury kept him from continuing to play so he decided to pursue coaching. He had been coaching when he was at Auburn and found he had a true passion for it.

He spent two years at the Alabama School of the Deaf between coaching stints because both of his parents were deaf and he wanted to fulfill a calling to help kids who suffered from deafness. He still had a love for coaching and returned to the sidelines and the baseball diamond at Tallassee.

Ronnie spent what he considers his most enjoyable time in coaching as an assistant to Shorty White at Banks from '66-'68. He coached the defense for White in the '66 and '67 seasons and was the head coach of the junior varsity.

"Shorty was a taskmaster," Baynes recalls. "There was never

anybody more dedicated who dotted his I's and crossed his T's. His weight program was way ahead of Auburn's when I was there. Everybody talks about the incredible athletes at Banks, but Shorty developed them. Johnny Musso is a good athlete (Baynes coached Musso). He was one of the slowest kids on the football team. Johnny was on the 440 relay team and he started ahead of everybody else but by the time he passed the baton he was five yards behind everybody. Shorty said Johnny was not going to run in any more track meets. He had incredible athletic ability and he loved it.

"Shorty made a bunch of sweet boys tough as you can get. We had Mike Neel and Phil Cochran who weighed 165 and 185 pounds and he made them very good. He built these blue collar kids. It was something to be a part of."

Banks didn't win a state championship in '66 or '67 but had fine football teams with Musso as the leader. Gary Rutledge was a sophomore on the '67 team and played quite a bit. Musso was also an outstanding baseball player and Baynes believes that Rutledge would have been drafted by the major leagues had he not opted to play football in college.

Baynes remembers the Ensley game, the Clinic game, in '67 as a huge game for the Banks program where Musso, Phares, and Rutledge led their team to victory. Banks rolled over Ensley in what White himself thought was a state championship caliber team by the end of the season. Sidney Lanier won it in '67.

Baynes recalls that White loved to bring out the blackboard and write up X's and O's though Ronnie does not think that was White's strong suit. For Baynes, it was White's ability to see potential and groom kids.

"He turned sweet boys into some of the toughest, finest young men on the football field who would knock your head off."

Baynes says that White, having been a boxer and having a tough upbringing, knew what it took to succeed through hard work and a demanding regimen for his players. But he also cared a lot for his boys.

"He had a lot of compassion for the kids. In the vernacular it was tough love. I can remember two sweet little boys, Bob Phares and Mike Neel, wrestling. They were the sweetest, nicest boys you'd ever want to meet. But I can remember those two going at each other and bleeding. It was amazing how he could develop these blue collar kids and make them so tough. His strength was his relationships with his players."

Though Baynes coached football at Talledega High School, he was legendary at baseball. One sportswriter called Baynes's baseball practices at Tallassee "Baseball Boot Camp." Ronnie is the first to admit he learned how to drive his players in practice from his experience with

White. It worked to the tune of five state titles in '86, '87, '89, '90 and '91.

Baynes remembers White as the strictest of disciplinarians not only with his players but also with his coaches.

"We were playing in the city championship against Ensley in a junior varsity game and Jim Currier and I were coaching the team. We were up by four or five points and we had the ball close to their goal line at the end of the game. We wanted to put it to Ensley because they were a big rival so we called a pass play. They intercepted it and ran it back 99 yards. Coach White came up to us the next day and he clenched his jaw and ground his teeth and all he said was, 'Who made the call?' We knew if one of us admitted it, we would probably lose our jobs so we both said we called it. We didn't think he could afford to fire both of us. He didn't. It wasn't one of my smarter moments.

"He was so committed. If you weren't as dedicated as he was, he would know it and you would not be in the job long. We had guys like Bobby Johns and David Cutcliffe and we loved it as much as he did. I loved coaching with him and I'm better off for having done so."

Baynes learned a little about integrity the Banks way during his time there. It was no surprise that Banks won the Sportsmanship Trophy for Birmingham City Schools in '66; that was something that White was most proud of along with the state championship in football in '65. White always emphasized sportsmanship to his players. He made this speech to the student body on their achievement after Banks received the award:

"As head football coach it is my responsibility to strive to instill in our athletes values such as character and leadership and to help them realize that these things are more important than just winning. One of the most important values is sportsmanship. Good sportsmanship demands honesty, a cooperative attitude, self-discipline, a competitive spirit and a desire to do what is right. A person does not have to be an athlete to practice sportsmanship. In fact, the non-athlete at Banks High School often has the better chance to show sportsmanship at an athletic contest. The Sportsmanship Trophy, which we received this year, symbolizes the sportsmanship that Banks already possesses. Let's let it serve as an incentive to build on our reputation as good sports, remembering that that's always the way to play the game."

White was a firm believer in playing the game to the best of one's ability and when it was over shaking the other man's hand, "and come back another Friday to try another day."

White had the full monty at Banks. He was an outstanding football coach, he had an outstanding staff, though there were only three coaches total at the time compared to staffs today that comprise seven or eight coaches, the parents were fully supportive, the school administration was behind White and believed in what he was doing and, his athletes were talented and, more importantly, willing to learn and give the ultimate effort. That's what White had at Banks that led to their dominance of 4A football, the highest classification, in the early 70's and had led to some highly successful seasons before in the mid- and late-60's.

White sees Hoover with 3,000 students as having an almost unfair advantage right now because of a large coaching staff, an exceptional group of athletes and unwavering support from parents and administration. White sees the situation as almost unfair and not as fun as it used to be because no one can compete with Hoover these days. There just isn't a sufficient student body population, though the coaching may be as good, at Vestavia Hills, Mountain Brook, Spain Park, Homewood, and Oak Mountain. "The larger the student body the more athletes there are," White says.

"When we were around, there would be schools like Woodlawn and Ensley that had the most students, over 1,000 in grades 9-12. Then there were the other city schools that had 750-800 students. It was close enough. Hoover has students for three schools. They've got the largest coaching staff in the state and the parents and the administration behind them. That's just a winning combination and that's all there is to it. As long as it stays that way they're going to be hard to beat. A team like Tuscaloosa County may sneak up on them like they did a couple of years ago, but there are 3,000 students there. You are supposed to win." Prattville changed that when they won 35-21 in the state championship game in 2006. Prattville has caught up.

There is talk of expanding to seven classes, meaning Hoover and the larger 6A schools would move to a higher class, leaving the smaller-enrollment 6A schools like Mountain Brook and Homewood competing in 6A, a better situation for them. White's favorite teams to watch are Vestavia Hills, Briarwood Christian—where his grandchildren have played and are playing, Mountain Brook and Homewood. Oak Mountain and Spain Park play good football as well.

White faced incredible competition in '65 and his team was more than competitive. They were dominant. The '65 team had a lot of special players and two of his favorites were Johnny Johnston and "The Moose," Johnny Musso, a sophomore. Musso is known by friends and former teammates as an unassuming, humble man. He has always been that way. White had started Johnston at running back until he got injured, then inserted Musso at tailback. When Johnston came back, White told Musso he was going to start Johnston because he wanted Johnston to get a scholarship.

"Musso said, 'I understand Coach,'" White recalls. "You couldn't upset him if you tried. He is one of a kind, he really is. If you have one come through like that in your career who has the attitude and the character and all plusses in all the areas, you are fortunate. I had more than one at Banks. We had some great kids."

White knew that character mattered on the football field because he knew he could trust his players to follow instructions and play to their utmost ability.

"I wanted them to be playing as hard in the fourth quarter as they did in the first," White stresses. "They may have gotten tired out there but it didn't show because we were in such great shape mentally and physically."

White says that in the city there may have been two of seven teams (Banks, Woodlawn, West End, Jones Valley, Ensley, Phillips and Ramsay) who were average or below average. "But the rest of the teams could whip you on any Friday night."

White contends there were coaches in Birmingham who haven't gotten the credit they deserve for what they accomplished in their careers. Coaches like Coach Tarrant, Ward Proctor at West End, and Ed Eubanks at Ramsay were men who got the most out of the talent they inherited every year.

White says that his bouts with Tandy Geralds, who coached Woodlawn in the early '70s and was the Colonels' coach in the famous Banks-Woodlawn duel in '74, were as tough as it got.

"They were hard-fought, close games. Those kids were like our kids. When we met on the field it was 'Pow!, Pow!' The kids were knocking the stew out of each other!"

White says that Bill Burgess was one of the best coaches this state has ever produced. "He always played the good guy at our practices while another coach and I would be the bad guy," White says. "The other two would be ripping through and he would be the good one. I couldn't be the good guy.

"The players loved him. Bill had a good career. At Oxford he never had a losing season. He was as hard-nosed as they come."

White would see the temperament of the team during practice and if anybody was slacking off or loafing he'd "jump 'em." White wanted everything done full speed and accepted nothing less. That's how his teams practiced, and how they played their games. There was no other gear except high throttle for Shorty.

"That was why we were strong in the fourth quarter. I told them you will be stronger at the end of the game. If you show up to practice every day and do what we ask you to do you will have a good chance at winning."

White loved his work and he says he had to, because the pay was not what it was in some of the smaller towns like Andalusia, Opelika, Dothan, Phenix City and Prattville and it was certainly not even close to what it is today with coaches at top programs making close to $100,000. That is not huge money but it's good money for doing what you love to do. White was making in the neighborhood of $20-$25,000/year if that much while teaching three or four academic classes. The academic load lightened in the later years at Banks when he was teaching only two classes.

"The Booster Club came through for me at the end and bought me a car," he says.

Lewis and Ruth Sidle, and Jimmy

Lewis and Ruth Sidle

Coach (left) and Jimmy

Coach (left), Jimmy, and Mother, Ruth Sidle

George O. White, Sr. (father)

Coach (left) and Mother, Ruth Sidle

Coach Running Against West End

Coach Running in Crippled Children's Classic

1947, Freshman Year at Phillips High School - Coach (41 at top left)

Birmingham Boys Club Boxing Team
Coach (bottom row, second from left)

Coach Running Track at Phillips High School

*Mr. and Mrs. Bill Anderson, and June (right)
at 1973 Cotton Bowl, Alabama vs. Texas*

Coach and June (1975)

*White Family Men (front row from left) Ramsey, Reagan, and Mike Barker
(rear row from left) Riley, Darryl, Coach, Gary, and Charlie*

*Gulf Shores Track Meet (from left) Darryl, Janice, Ramsey,
Chaney, Riley, Reagan, Coach, and June*

Coach at Alabama Sports Hall of Fame, 1965 State Champions Reunion

Coach and June

White Family Portrait
(top row) Mike Barker, Darryl, Janice, and Gary
(2nd row) Riley, Jaymie, Dianne Barker, Ramsey, and Cecelia
(3rd row) Coach, June, and Chaney
(bottom row) Charlie, Brittney, Brooke, and Reagan

CHAPTER 11
Golden Years (1972-1973)

After some solid years in the late '60s and early '70s, White saw his '72 team as having the best chance of winning the state championship since his '65 team. And he was prophetic. The '72 Jets team rolled through the season outscoring their opponents 346-96. Jeff Rutledge was emerging as one of the top quarterbacks in the state if not the nation. He was just a sophomore. And there were plenty of other players. Off the '72 team, Johnny Gunnels, Fred Dawson, Danny Collins and Danny Neal all got football scholarships to Alabama. Running back Rodney Johnson got a scholarship to Georgia, Gary Gustin got a scholarship to play at Auburn and Ricky Morrow, who was also an outstanding basketball player, earned a scholarship to Arkansas for football.

Banks started out the season rolling over Carver 56-0. Then came city rival Ramsay and their standout quarterback Chris Vacarella, leading the city in total yardage, rushing and passing. White's team shut Vacarella and Ramsay down 42-0. Then, an always difficult game against Berry. With one of the top coaches in the state in Bob Finley, Berry played White and Banks almost to a draw with the Jets surviving 6-2.

White has a lot of admiration for Finley. "He was a good man and a good football coach." Banks then defeated Mountain Brook (21-7), Ensley (41-19), Jones Valley (19-0), Huffman (23-6), tied Berry in the Clinic Game (14-14) and went into the playoffs ready to advance and grab a state title. That they did.

They opened the playoffs in a game with Davidson of Mobile and were tied at the end of regulation 20-20. Joe Shaw, a standout defensive player for the Jets who was also the kicker, had missed a kick that would have won the game. But he came back with a vengeance in overtime. In '72, the ball was placed at the 50 in overtime and each team had four plays to gain as many yards as possible. The team that gained the most yards was the winner. Davidson Coach Glen Yancey won the toss of the coin and elected to take the ball.

Shaw was all over the Davidson backfield. "Joe Shaw was knocking those guys on their fanny. He was not going to lose the game. They lost yards and I told our kids to hold onto that ball and cross the line of scrimmage."

Banks came away with the victory and a lot of confidence. White did not like that way of settling a game.

"I like to put the ball on the 25, get four snaps and then give the other team a whack at it."

White's team went on to shut out Tuscaloosa 21-0 to earn a spot in the state championship against city rival Huffman. A week before Huffman beat Number 1 Jeff Davis of Montgomery using a spread formation offense. "Before that game we added the 4-3 defense that is used today," White says. "It was the difference in the game." It was the first time two teams from Birmingham had played in the state title game, instituted in 1966 the year after White and Banks won their first state title as voted by the Alabama Sports Writers.

Banks blasted Huffman 34-8. Jeff Rutledge was 7-of-10 passing for 148 yards with a touchdown of 36 yards to receiver Steve Grefseng. Johnny Gunnels carried 18 times for 71 yards and Rodney Johnson added 57 yards on 16 totes. The defense led by Freddie Knighton, Joe Shaw, Danny Neal, Frank Deliz and Jobie Frame allowed a meager four yards rushing and 10 yards passing and intercepted Huffman three times. Tommy Saffles, Rick Neal and Danny Beck had interceptions for the Jets.

White says that it was a fulfilling experience for him competitively and for his kids, whom he had great admiration for.

"There was a lot of character on that team. You couldn't ask for a better disciplined group. They would give you whatever effort it took."

Fred Dawson, one of White's standouts at offensive tackle, had always wanted to get a shot at playing fullback to carry the ball. He was 6-2, 220 so he certainly had the size to take a lick and pass one out. He asked White if he would put him in at fullback. White told him that if the team scored 30 points, he would put him in. When Banks put over 30 on the board, Dawson asked White again. White gave him a shot. He got the call and, according to White, "He got the living daylights knocked out of him. He got drilled. He came up to me after that and said, 'Coach, I want to stay at offensive tackle!'"

Banks finished the season 12-0-1 and began a dynasty that would be forever linked to high school football in Alabama.

For Danny Collins, a key member of the '72 team who went on to start at Alabama, those were special times.

"It was a bonding experience. Coach White was an old-fashioned coach who had self-imposed rules for the players. We might not have liked it at the time, but I really appreciate it now. You knew you were part of something special. He is most deserving of getting in the Alabama Sports Hall of Fame. He is an amazing guy."

Joe Shaw says that White was second to none in his ability to lead young men.

"I have said this before, I went on to play at Auburn and I played Little League for 12 years, and Coach White was the best coach I ever played for. He was not the easiest. When we were freshmen we started out with 107 people. Coach Larry Ferris lined us up in single file on the practice field and had us pick up rocks for 30 minutes and then run wind sprints. There were 65 people left by the time the season started and 45 people at the end of the season. It was an incredible work ethic on that team.

"Most young people couldn't relate today. Coach White wanted to win badly but he wanted to do so in a fair and right way. He made us be the best we could be. There were a lot of stories about Freddie Knighton on our team. At 15, he was a grown man. He intimidated everybody. Coach White wanted us all to be our best. He said if we gave it our best effort, we would be satisfied with the result."

Tommy Saffles echoes his former teammates' assessments of White.

"He was extremely strong. He was an extreme disciplinarian. He was like a college coach. He was a CEO and he got good assistants and let them coach. He taught us to be leaders. He taught us to be efficient in all phases of the game. He spent as much time on special teams as he did first-team defense. Those are still some of the best memories of my life along with my wife and kids.

"Coach White would say to us, 'I don't care what you do, just be the best you can be at whatever profession you choose.' He was a stickler for having the locker room spotless, having your headgear in the right place in your locker, your jerseys and your socks in the right place. He wanted that locker room perfectly straight. He was the ultimate professional. He and that team will always be a part of my life."

White remembers after the Berry game in 1973, a year after Berry had tied the Jets 14-14, the only blemish on an otherwise perfect state championship season, he was checking everyone's lockers after the game. Banks had just demolished Berry 35-6 and Knighton had knocked Berry's star tailback John Turpin out of the game on a clean hit. Turpin and his backfield mate had called themselves Csonka and Kiick after Larry Csonka and Jim Kiick, the famous running backs for the Miami Dolphins. "We Csonka and Kicked them," White quips. Knighton went through two linemen for Berry to hit Turpin; one went on to play football at Alabama and another was a state heavyweight champion wrestler at Alabama. When White checked the lockers he noticed that Knighton's headgear was out of place. White was putting Knighton's helmet back in the right place, ready to scold him for not having it properly in his locker when he noticed a picture in Knighton's helmet. It was a picture of Turpin. White came up to him later and Knighton told Shorty, "Coach, I'm sorry about my headgear. I was so tired."

To White, Knighton "was the toughest kid who ever played for me."

The '73 squad was awesome on both sides of the ball. They outscored their opponents 337-122. They were 13-0, winning the state championship game over Grissom 21-0. White lost Rutledge in the first game of the playoffs against Wenonah, a 35-19 Banks victory. Rutledge had his wrist broken in the game. "It was not a clean hit, they were hitting him late all game. He was scared to death." But White's team prevailed. On the bus ride home, one of the players sang, "United we stand, divided we fall." White says it gave him confidence. "I told the coaches if we coach this team right we can win this thing."

The next week the Jets played Butler in the second round, a team that averaged 268 pounds across its defensive line. White started his son Gary at quarterback. White called an outside Veer play and realized right before the play that Gary was going to get killed when he ran that play. White was screaming for a timeout but the offense didn't hear him. "Gary got knocked out cold as a wedge," White remembers. White used Rick Neal at quarterback. Neal was efficient enough and the defense took care of the rest as the Jets prevailed 8-6. White enjoyed beating the Butler coach, who had a very high opinion of himself. He called Shorty over before the game and had nothing to say to him. White didn't know what he wanted and said, "I've got a team to coach and I'm not going to waste any more time here. If you need anything, let me know." White and his players then took care of business. The next week, the Jets went up to Huntsville to face Grissom and shut them out, winning the state championship 21-0.

"It was another special year with a group of kids who had a lot of character and were highly disciplined," White reminisces. "Banks was a great place to be. Those were golden years."

Ike McDonald, the team chaplain for Banks in the early '70s

concurs. McDonald admires White immensely and appreciates that his approach to the game and his players was one of complete dedication and commitment.

"I never saw him raise his voice to a particular player. He was a master motivator and took a great interest in the kids. He would see a kid who was having a problem and he would ask me if I would have a talk with him.

"He was so precise in everything he did. He was a gentlemen also, a prince of a guy."

McDonald is 75 now and lives in Elizabethtown, Kentucky for most of the year and Venice, Florida during the winter. He is of course a big follower of Kentucky football and basketball.

Another man of faith who appreciates Shorty's spirituality is Pete Clifford, an old bud of White's, having known him at Phillips High School; Pete also served as the team chaplain while White was at Banks.

Clifford went to Birmingham-Southern where he played tennis before being called for service in the armed forces. He was in the 11th Airborne Division of the Army in what is today the Special Forces Rangers. They operated secret missions.

He did not serve in active combat but was a point man for public information. He was also in excellent shape, able to run five miles a day with an Army pack on his back.

In the early 50's during the Korean War, Clifford had a special mission he participated in, whereby the Army made it public that they were going to perform a military exercise in Alaska. The soldiers were supposedly flying from Fort Campbell, Kentucky, where Clifford and the Airborne Division were based, to Fort Ord, Washington. The 11th Airborne was actually trying to rescue a marine division in South Korea. So instead of going to Alaska, Pete's division flew to Japan, then went on to Korea where they rescued the division.

Clifford came back to Birmingham and graduated from Birmingham-Southern, then received a scholarship to attend Emory University's seminary. He graduated from Emory in 1958 and after serving a brief time in Atlanta at a Methodist Church, he returned to Birmingham and started as minister of the Forest Hills Methodist Church in Fairfield. After spending time at Forest Hills, then Trinity Methodist Church in Homewood, Clifford settled in at Wilson Chapel Methodist Church in Huffman in 1960. His mission: grow the church.

He grew the church from 99 members to 850. He reunited with White, who wanted to start a Fellowship of Christian Athletes chapter. Clifford calls the Banks kids, "the finest kids I knew"; they regularly attended church and came to pray on weeknights and even on Saturdays.

White asked Clifford to be the chaplain of the football team. Not only was Clifford inspirational to White and the players, he took an active role in practices. He would hold blocking dummies while players practiced their blocking drills. He would also run and work out with them. Pete took a special interest in the players.

"One time Billy Strickland didn't do something right on the field during the game, he came off the field and he was berating himself," Clifford remembers. "I came up to him and I shook my finger and told him to suck it up and do the very best he could. He got back in the game and did marvelously well."

The Fellowship of Christian Athletes chapter that White and Clifford established was a booming success at Banks.

Clifford was very close to Johnny Musso. He recalls going over to Musso's house when Musso was at Banks and noticing a big bowl and a small bowl of lasagna on the table. Clifford thought the big bowl was for everybody, but it was strictly for the Moose. Pete says he and the family divided up the other bowl.

"I would go down to see the boys who played at Banks when they were in college," Clifford says. "I would go to Alabama, Auburn and Georgia Tech among others. I went to Alabama to see Johnny, studying at his desk and I thought I'd say something smart, like, 'you'd better be studying.' Johnny came up and gave me a big hug and said, 'I've got to study, I'm making a C in a course and my mother is going to kill me.' Here was a back who was running over defensive players throughout the Southeastern Conference and he was most afraid of his mother seeing a C on his report card.

"We went down to eat dinner in the chow hall and Johnny got me to get the lasagna and he got two steaks because that's what the coaches wanted him to eat. He ended up switching with me because he wanted lasagna."

Clifford says that White wasn't one to quote Scripture but he lived his life as a model to his players. "He was a special guy, Banks was a special place and it was a special team. He never got on his coaches in front of me or the players. He always encouraged them. When he wanted to tell his players something like how to block on the line he would always show them. Shorty took a special interest in the kids." Clifford is now the pastor at Independent Methodist Church in Huffman and assistant to the President at Southeastern Bible College. He is 78 years old and looks like he's in his late 60's. He had a passion for Banks

High School and the players and students.

"It's still such an influence on my life 47 years later. I trust it's the same for Shorty White and the boys he coached."

One of Shorty's most trusted coaches to help him with his boys was Robert Higginbotham, a huge name in Alabama high school coaching, tops in the business for 35 years. He had his teams in the state championship mix for many of those years at Mountain Brook, Shades Valley and now at Tuscaloosa County. Higginbotham won the state championship at Mountain Brook in 1975 with Major Ogilvie at tailback.

Higginbotham played for his father, Morris Higginbotham at Hueytown. (Morris Higginbotham is in the Alabama High School Hall of Fame.) Son Robert then played for Bear Bryant at Alabama and went into high school coaching at Etowah County. After a season at Etowah County and a four-month military obligation, Higginbotham had some options in high school coaching. He had a chance to go back to Etowah County, take a job in Huntsville or come to Banks and work with Shorty White. Higginbotham accepted White's offer and took over the Banks defense in 1972.

As defensive coordinator at Banks, Higginbotham helped the Jets win the state championship. White let him coach the defense while he focused on the offense and Higginbotham used some of the talent Banks had to help lead the Jets to a 12-0-1 record and a 34-8 victory over Huffman in the state title game. Banks only allowed seven and a half points per game in that season.

"It was a great experience working with Shorty," Higginbotham says. "He's not in the Hall of Fame but he certainly will get in there."

Higginbotham used his experience with White to launch his own head coaching career. After the '72 season, he was offered the position of head coach at Mountain Brook where in three years he built a state championship program.

"I didn't know anything about offense when I got to Banks but I learned about the split back Veer from Coach White and that was one of the biggest things he taught me."

Higginbotham had weapons like Freddie Knighton and brothers Danny and Rick Neal, all stellar players on defense at Banks. Knighton was a dominant 175-pound defensive tackle and Higginbotham noticed before the season that his sophomore was better than the senior who was 6-4, 250; he told White about him.

"I told Coach White before the season that Freddie was better than the guy in front of him and Coach said, 'put him in there'. He started and wound up getting a scholarship to Alabama."

Higginbotham says not only was White great with his weight program but also with his willingness to learn. Higginbotham points to White's going out to the University of Houston and learning their offense from Bill Yeomen.

Robert notes that Banks also used a conditioning program patterned after Alabama's, the three-ring circuit, an intense conditioning program that tested players' physical and mental toughness.

"Coach Bryant used it in 1966—we had already done it at Banks—not to the extent that Alabama used it, but it was pretty tough and pretty demanding for those kids."

Higginbotham had a great relationship with White and still does today.

"He went out of his way to help me out and he was always very nice to me. He was a big part of my getting the job at Mountain Brook."

Higginbotham remembers White as "meticulous." He was all about getting jerseys, helmets, shoulder pads and shoes in order.

"Coach White was big on the helmets and one time we had a guy put a Jet on the helmet with smoke coming out. Coach White didn't think there was enough smoke coming out of the helmet so he made the guy do it over."

For Higginbotham, a Banks-Hoover matchup today would be tough to judge, to see which team was better.

"It's hard to compare eras. I know we had a lot of guys going both ways back then and Hoover doesn't have to do that. We had three coaches and they have ten to twelve. I know Banks won the state in '72 and '73 and there is no doubt in my mind they would have won the state in '74 if Jeff Rutledge had not gotten hurt in the last game of the regular season."

Danny Newman might just agree with that analysis. One of White's closest friends and advocates since they were young boys, Danny served as president of the Booster Club at Banks in '73. Danny remembers White as always being a tough guy. "I was scared to be around him; all he used to talk about was football and fighting." Newman remembers playing tackle football on the pavement near Legion Field and White throwing him seven or eight touchdown passes when they played the sons of the Birmingham-Southern College professors, who lived in College Hills, an affluent suburb.

Newman calls White "a strict disciplinarian" when he coached football at Banks. Newman says that White would get his players on a weight program and have them take vitamins; he motivated them to love to play football.

After Banks beat Butler 8-6 in the semifinal game of the 4A playoffs in '73, the Grissom coach, whose team would face Banks in the state championship game, said, "If we can't beat Banks there's not a cow in the state!" Banks went on to beat Grissom 21-0 and the coach for Grissom sent White a steak.

Newman recalls White had very physical practices and that one of his players died from playing bull in the ring, a common practice drill featuring one player in the middle and other players around him in a circle. The coach calls out a number and a player who is part of the circle lays a hit on the guy in the middle. Tragically, a player under White died from that drill. "That really hurt Shorty," Newman says. "He never got over that."

Danny thinks the biggest influence in White's life was Ms. Allen, his elementary school teacher who took him up to varsity football practices at Phillips in spring of his eighth grade year. She always encouraged him to be the best he could be. In '74 when White got a new Ford car from the Booster Club, he and June drove to Georgia to see Ms. Allen.

A teacher and cheerleading coach at Banks named Mrs. Elizabeth Hatch locked horns with White at times. "She was equally as good with the girls as he was on the football field," Newman recalls. Her cheerleading squads swept the state championships from '72-'74. One time White's punter unintentionally hit a girl in the head with a punt when the cheerleading squad was on the field during practice.

The key characteristic that White had as a coach, according to Danny, was that all the players loved him. "He was honest. When he had something on his mind you couldn't change him if he thought it was right. And he was a very determined individual."

White also enjoyed a lot of support. Newman recalls that one major supporter of the Banks football program physically built the football practice field. White also inspired a group to help him build the weight house, which White played a major role in building, hands-on.

CHAPTER 12
42,000 Strong (1974)

Winning streaks end eventually, but the journey to excel never ends.

Shorty White put together one of the more remarkable winning streaks in Alabama high school football history and he had a solid, disciplined, academically sound program to go along with it. The man did it right.

West End defeated Banks 35-27 on November 15, 1974 to end Banks' 25-game winning streak and a streak of 35 games without a loss from 1972-1974.

White's legacy was greatness both on and off the field. He shaped young men into first-class citizens and his football resumé at Banks spoke for itself : state championships in 1965, 1972 and 1973. But for Jeff Rutledge's broken ankle against West End, Banks would have likely won another state title in 1974. White went to the University of Alabama in 1975 and excelled in Tuscaloosa. He was on a staff that won national championships in 1978 and 1979 under Bear Bryant.

But this memoir is not only about White's fine football career, it's about the man and what shaped him and how he shaped the people around him. It's also the story of Birmingham during White's life, what was going on in society and what the culture was like in the 1930's, 40's, 50's, 60's and early 70's.

Today, White lives in thriving Helena, a growing metropolis in Shelby County, south of Birmingham, full of cul-de-sacs and upper middle class areas. White has a two-story brick house he shares with his lovely wife, June, who when I interviewed the coach, would always fix a fantastic lunch and show the utmost interest in this book and, of course, in her husband. Shorty has a great woman behind him, that's for certain.

You meander up the stairs to Shorty's den and you see a wall that's covered with high school football memorabilia. Shorty's 1965, '72 and '73 state championships are recorded in framed pictures with the schedule and final scores, the roster of players and a picture of an animated Banks football player. The Coach has books and movies galore; June "watches the movies." White watches football and the news on his huge TV. He's up to date on what's happening in the world.

He showed me film clips from the 1974 season in which Jeff Rutledge put on a show before his unfortunate injury in the West End game. The Coach and I would be watching film and when Rutledge would zip a pass to receivers Bob Grefseng or Jerry McDonald, White would intone "Zoom!" or "Whoom!" His enthusiasm for the game was contagious; I found myself amazed at the abilities of these Banks football teams. White was a coach ahead of his time. He had a sophisticated pass offense before there was such a thing. His teams looked like the 49ers with Montana and Rice or the Cowboys with Aikman and Irvin. It was great entertainment.

Back in 1974, White's juggernaut was demolishing the opposition, averaging 43 points per game through the first eight games of the season. The scores of the victories tell the story of this football powerhouse : Banks 62, Carver 0; Banks 71, Hayes 0; Banks 42, Ramsay 0; Banks 49, Mountain Brook 12; Banks 28, Berry 7; Banks 45, Ensley 7; Banks 35, Huffman 0; Banks 35, Jones Valley 7 and Banks 18, Woodlawn 7.

Jeff Rutledge, who had led Banks to their '72 and '73 state championships, was an All-American quarterback for the Jets with playmakers all around him: Jerry Murphree, the hard-nosed, talented tailback, McDonald at wide receiver and Grefseng at tight end. Running against the Banks defense was like running into a fortified concrete wall; you weren't going very far. The defense allowed only four points per game through the first nine games of '74.

After an intensely satisfying but highly competitive and physical victory over Woodlawn and All-America tailback Tony Nathan, Banks was beaten up on defense, having lost two starters in that game. They then lost another player on defense in practice that week. Randy Duke, a two-year starter at defensive tackle, of whom White remarked, "we didn't know how much we lost losing him," was knocked out after the Woodlawn game. Linebacker Greg Muse, who, according to White, had great feet, could run like a gazelle and was also a defensive mainstay, was also lost for the upcoming game against 9-0 West End. The Lions were an outstanding team in their own right with one of the better coaches in the state, Ray Williams.

Grefseng, the Jets' standout tight end/linebacker, had mononucleosis but didn't tell White and played against West End. The sharp-eyed White had noticed he had lost weight the week of the game.

Banks faced a monumental challenge when they squared off with West End on November 15, 1974. The Lions, of course, were homing in on upsetting one of the top high school programs in the country and ending the two-time defending state champions' reign at the top of Alabama High School football, ending the 35-game unbeaten streak.

White had prepared his team thoroughly that week as usual, but he had concerns. First was the quality of the opponent. Second was how his team would react after such an emotional and hard-fought victory. But White knew his boys would be ready to play. That was Banks football.

Then, with Banks moving the football in the first quarter, the worst possible scenario White could anticipate—which he always did in the back of his mind—occurred. Rutledge went down with an injury on a pass play. Rutledge's ankle was broken. Jeff was upset and in tears. White said, "I was worn out, so fatigued and that was just too much, I tried to keep a positive outlook, but it was difficult. Then I looked at my players' faces and there was no quit in them. We were not going to go down without a tremendous fight."

Gary White, Shorty's son, took over at quarterback. He gave a tremendous effort but West End prevailed 35-27.

White was so upset after the game that he couldn't talk to *The Birmingham News* reporter.

"It was somebody I had never talked to," he said. "They usually had Wayne Martin or Ronald Weathers who covered us all the time, but they were at other games. I just couldn't talk to the guy. I was too depressed and worn out. This was not a wise decision. I should have been more courteous."

Still Banks was in the playoffs. The players sang, "United We Stand" on the bus ride back to school. There was no quit in the Banks football team. They had accomplished too much and there was so much pride among the players.

Banks played Homewood the following week in the playoffs at Legion Field. Gary White was the starting quarterback for the game but missed the first three days of school and practice with a bad virus. White told his son on Thursday that if he didn't attend class he wouldn't play. Gary practiced and played.

"If Gary hadn't been sick all week I think we would have had a good chance of winning," White muses. "They had a good defense and an excellent kicker. They only scored one touchdown, missed the extra point and kicked two field goals. Our defense didn't play well against West End and our offense didn't perform against Homewood. Still Homewood won the state championship that year, so I felt ok about that."

There were memorable moments earlier in the year. In the Wenonah game, White remembers that Jerry Murphree had one of the most beautiful runs he had ever seen. Murphree, who ran for 140 yards for the game, "broke three tackles and carried a couple of guys in the end zone. He got hit three times and he refused to go down," White says. "He was on one leg when he went into the end zone."

White regrets the way he felt after the Rutledge injury.

"I was usually pretty good at getting kids up, but I really felt like I let them down," he recalls.

White's 1974 team, he thought, would have the best chance of winning the state. He felt like they could excel in the playoffs because of their ability to score.

"I was so worn out and disgusted after the West End game I couldn't talk," he says.

Banks had recently integrated the school and there were two black players on the '74 team, Milton Miles and Kenny Cooper. Both knocked on White's door after the season and told White what he had meant to them.

"They said, 'Coach, we wanted to tell you how much we appreciated playing for Banks High School and Shorty White.' I gave 'em both a hug."

The streak was over and after the season, White accepted a job from Bear Bryant as his offensive backs coach, where he would coach players like Major Ogilvie, Tony Nathan, Steve Whitman, Willie Shelby, James Taylor, Lou Ikner, and Johnny Davis, and become part of the 1978 and 1979 national championship teams. But White had his greatest experience in high school.

"In college if you won it was like another day in the office, there was not as much fun. I missed the thrill we got out of winning."

His players were always serious on the football field.

"There were never any characters on that team, we were serious. I didn't know what was going on in the country or the world. I was concerned about winning the next game," Shorty observes.

His players were serious, but they did enjoy the victories.

"The players were hootin' and hollerin' after games. I tried to calm them down, but they got excited."

Without the injuries in '74, Banks most likely could have captured its third state title and kept the winning streak alive.

"Winning streaks do get broken, I knew it couldn't last forever. Records are made to be broken," White says. "I thought Hoover was going to break our streak, but they were beaten by Tuscaloosa County. That Robert Higginbotham is a winner."

Higginbotham, the Tuscaloosa County coach, was defensive coordinator for White at Banks in 1972 before taking the Mountain Brook job, where he won the state championship in 1975.

"Robert figured out Huffman's offense before the 1972 title game. He's one of my favorite coaches along with Dyer Carlisle and Bill Burgess."

Carlisle is now principal at Homewood, a high school football powerhouse of this millennium and a fine high school above and beyond that. Burgess won the Division 2 national championship at Jacksonville State in 1992.

Banks had great crowds at Legion Field, the Football Mecca of the South in the 1960's and 70's. Twenty thousand people would show up to watch Banks play on Friday nights during the winning streak. And Rutledge was a phenom.

Coach White showed me film of Rutledge in games in '74. We saw Rutledge throw one of his darts to a receiver and White would say, "Zoom, Boom!" It was an impressive show. White was a coach ahead of his time and Rutledge was also a quarterback ahead of his time. Both would flourish in this millennium if White could get the cooperation of the kids that he had in the 70's. He made sure he kept his players in line back then.

"We did not need to do much to keep them motivated because they were good students. They stayed on their work."

White's militaristic approach to his profession worked with his players, who were dedicated to Banks High School and to their football team.

"We had smart kids," White said. "Bob Grefseng was in the National Honor Society. Jeff Rutledge. Gary, Jeff's older brother (who played at Alabama), was very smart. These were good kids. The 70's players were the last of the guys who could take the tough practices. This is before players got soft. It changed after the 70's."

White lost his last game as a high school football coach but his legacy was cemented in high school history. With over 88 players who received college scholarships and three state titles, White's proven excellence and his strong leadership are lessons for today's coaches who still teach discipline but have to back off because of more sensitive kids and parents.

White left an indelible mark on high school football from 1961-1974 at Banks. It's a legacy that needs to be told.

One of the players who tells it best is Jeff Rutledge. Jeff was on three Super Bowl teams: the Los Angeles Rams in 1980, the New York Giants in 1987 and the Washington Redskins in 1992. Two of those teams won Super Bowls: the Giants and the Redskins. He was also the quarterback and leader of Alabama's 1979 national championship team.

With all those successes on the football field Rutledge's favorite athletic memories are from high school, playing at Banks for Shorty White.

"I played at the highest level and played for some great coaches but I had the most fun in my three years in high school," Rutledge smiles.

Rutledge says that Coach White was "tough," but he also cared for the well-being of his players and served as a father figure to many of his boys.

Jeff remembers a commitment among him and his teammates, a camaraderie and dedication to excellence that made the Banks teams achieve greatness when he played starting quarterback from '71-'74. That commitment, and closeness that the team had, led to state championships in '72 and '73 and another great season in '74 when Banks had a terrific shot at winning its third straight until Rutledge went down in the last game of the season. Banks had not been defeated in 35 games—34 wins and one tie—until the 35-27 loss to West End at the end of '74.

Rutledge recalls that he and his teammates all had summer jobs so they'd work eight hours, then go work out, condition, throw and catch at Banks. White expected them there and would not allow them to skip.

"I worked a construction job for eight hours a day and then I'd go work out with Coach White. If you missed you were going to get a phone call and Shorty would say, 'Where are you? Get down here.'"

Rutledge learned discipline and commitment from his dad, Jack Rutledge, who he says stayed on him and his older brother Gary about their work ethic and committing to everything they participated in. A little known fact is Gary and Jeff are the only brothers to have won national championships as quarterbacks. (Gary, in 1973, and Jeff, in 1979.)

Rutledge instilled that commitment in his players as coach of Montgomery Bell Academy in Nashville where he won state championships in football in 2002 and 2003. Montgomery Bell played in Division 2 football in Tennessee, nine private schools that play the best football in the state.

Rutledge has now moved on to the NFL as quarterbacks coach

for the Arizona Cardinals where he is tutoring former USC Heisman Trophy winner Matt Leinart.

Jeff says that his dad and White had a great relationship.

"My dad would always speak his mind," Rutledge recalls. "He would ask Coach White, "Why didn't you throw the football earlier in the game? We would have won if you'd have thrown more!" Rutledge says his dad was not afraid to express his opinions to Coach Bryant either at Alabama.

Jeff Rutledge got his first chance to play quarterback his freshman year at Banks in a game against Phillips when his team was trailing 14-0 at halftime. White called on Rutledge in the second half.

"We had lost a game the week before and Coach White had us run, the whole practice, the following Monday. We were doing up-downs and running sprints the whole practice, we didn't run a play. I was at the beginning of the line and I thought when I got to the end of the line I was through, I wasn't coming back. I didn't have anything to do with our loss the week before, and I was going through this? When I was almost to the end of the line Coach blew the whistle and practice was over. He came over to me and said, "I wanted to see how you responded. Then he put me in against Phillips. David Cutcliffe was on the offensive line and he told me, "I believe in you, believe in yourself."

Rutledge led the team to a comeback 15-14 victory over Phillips and began an outstanding career on the high school level that culminated in Banks's resounding 18-7 victory over Woodlawn and superstar Tony Nathan at Legion Field before 42,000 fans in November, 1974.

"Coach had given me and the players a gut check. He was tough. You either did it his way or you weren't going to play."

White would see Rutledge and another player talking to a girl on game day and he would grab them by the arm and take them to class. "That was just Coach White," Jeff laughs.

Rutledge notes that the coaching he got in high school prepared him better for Alabama than that of most other players who went to Tuscaloosa.

"He had such a great knowledge of the game. He was just a heckuva football coach."

Rutledge says that it is hard to compare the Banks team of '74 with some of the Hoover teams of this decade that have won multiple state championships. Rutledge does note that there were eight players off the '74 team who received SEC scholarships, a total not equaled on the high school level in Alabama since.

"We had guys like Jerry McDonald, Freddie Knighton and me

who got scholarships to Alabama, Jerry Murphree who got a scholarship to LSU and Joe Shaw who got a scholarship at Auburn. We were a close group. Hoover's style of play is totally different from how we played. They're wide open but they haven't had eight guys from one class who signed SEC scholarships."

Rutledge was demanding of his players at Montgomery Bell and is now that way at Arizona but he didn't have the ability to get his players in until August in Tennessee for two-a-day practices.

"With all this AAU basketball and baseball, it is harder. Back then, in the early 70's, football in Alabama started June 1st."

Rutledge has the insight that despite the fact that White was demanding, and a strict disciplinarian who was tough on his players, there was something else about him that separated him from coaches solely focused on winning.

"You knew he truly cared about you. You didn't want to disappoint him. He'd chew you out but you knew he was out for your best interest."

Rutledge says that in the early 70's you had to win 13 games without a loss to win the state championship. What his group accomplished is almost unprecedented.

"The thing I remember most is how much fun I had playing high school football. We were just a committed, dedicated group who always thought about winning the state championship every year and under Coach White we did twice."

Jeff last saw White at his dad's funeral and they renewed their friendship. "He's always friendly and nice. The thing that was amazing about him was that he did it all. He taped ankles, kept the field up, washed clothes and coached both sides of the football. He was also the weight coach. At Montgomery Bell I had three coaches for weights on my staff."

White was the ultimate coach, according to Rutledge, and most importantly, was in it for his players. The spectacular record achieved by Rutledge speaks for itself: two high school state championships, one national championship ring, and a pair of Super Bowl rings. The man knows what it takes to win.

Another winner groomed by Shorty is Bob Grefseng. Bob was a standout linebacker and sometimes tight end on the Banks teams that won the state championship in '73 and finished 9-2 in '74. Grefseng along with six other Banks players earned Division One football scholarships in '75. Grefseng was a three-year starter at linebacker for Ole Miss.

Grefseng grew up watching Banks football and was in awe of what for him as a youngster was, "big-time football."

Shorty White was a legend already in Alabama coaching circles and Grefseng found out why once he suited up for White.

"We were walking on pins and needles all the time around him. He had that persona about him and God, it was effective."

Bob remembers two-a-days at Birmingham Industrial School near Banks as rigorous.

"We only got two breaks and that was with crushed ice. You couldn't do that today. He was like Bear Bryant and all the legendary coaches where you know who is boss and you deliver or you're in trouble. The reason we won so much is because we were afraid of losing."

And Grefseng says that White was the ultimate leader and a man whose teaching ability has stuck with Bob throughout his life.

"Coach White did teach principles I have used that have paid off later in life. You got a good lesson on what hard work can do for you. I was much more prepared for college and adult life. He demanded excellence and would not accept anything less."

Grefseng remembers a specific example of White's driven nature during the '74 season.

"We were preparing for a game with Berry early in the season. Berry I think was number one in the state at the time. We had played Carver and some other teams earlier in the year that we had beaten easily. We beat our brains out that week of practice. It was hot and Coach was saying that if we play like we've been practicing, Berry will embarrass us. He said that it was going to be awful.

"We were like a bunch of caged animals let loose. We beat Berry every which way and knocked their fullback out. I don't know if Coach thought we were really that bad that week or if he was using some kind of manipulation. I don't know what Berry's ultimate record was but they didn't have a good showing against us, Banks won 28-7. We were fully prepared."

Grefseng played linebacker most of the time, but did get some chances at tight end his senior year.

"I remember in the '74 Woodlawn game I caught a touchdown pass. Jeff threw three passes to me and I caught all three of them. I liked my stats in high school."

Bob mainly played inside linebacker with Frankie Gunnells, who signed with the University of Georgia.

Grefseng, who coached some high school football and Little League for his son's team, is now a lawyer in Columbia, Tennessee. He says that there is a big difference between playing and coaching.

"Playing is easy—getting others to do it is more difficult. I have to compliment Coach White and the other coaches. They made excellent use of the talent we had. We had the right personnel. We went 35 games without a loss so he was doing something right."

Grefseng asserts that White knew exactly how to instill respect in his players for him.

"He was a tremendous motivator. I feared the guy. If I was walking the hall and I knew he was walking my way, I would go around. He was never insulting or demeaning, but all business all the time. By the force of his will he made a lot of our teams successful. I loved football, I loved playing and wouldn't trade playing on any of those teams for anything."

Bob goes on to say that he developed a tremendous camaraderie with his teammates, his best friends for life. White emphasized teamwork and the players bonded in an attempt to survive practices.

"He always seemed to be able to say the right things. I can remember him saying we represented our school, our families and our community. Those things hit home with me. If he had told us to line up in front of a brick wall and run as hard as you can, we would have done that because he said to do it. He had that much influence. There was a desire to please him."

Grefseng says that White was the master at teaching fundamentals. He focused on the offense but Bob's defensive coaches echoed White's emphasis on fundamentals.

"It was everybody getting to the ball. It was about swarming to the ball and gang tackling. We were bigger, stronger and faster before that was in vogue. Football was a year-round deal. We practiced as hard in two-a-days as anywhere I ever did."

Grefseng caught on as a free agent for the Seattle Seahawks but still says that White's practices were the most intense of any Bob was a part of.

"Starting three years at Ole Miss I attribute completely to the quality of high school football in Alabama. We were way ahead at Banks."

Grefseng was 6-2 and about 200 pounds his senior year at Banks, which didn't have an intimidating team size-wise, but the effort and determination they put forth in practice and games made them the elite program in Alabama.

"On offense it was execution. The quarterbacks and backs ran plays time after time. It was precision. Our backs were quick so the linemen held their blocks and the backs were through the hole. Jeff Rutledge was a real good quarterback. He made all the right reads. On defense we stressed gang tackling, everybody getting to the ball playing sideline to sideline."

Grefseng is highly appreciative of his high school coach.

"The discipline I learned from playing for Coach White has paid great dividends. I learned that nothing is free. You have to earn it. You were prepared to perform. I learned that from Coach White."

One of the most talented, ferocious and decorated performers White ever coached was Freddie Knighton. Knighton had an innate work ethic, tremendous courage and a fierce competitive will and toughness that made him one of the best football players in the state from '72 to '74.

White loved Knighton and Knighton had an equal admiration and love for his coach and does to this day. He respects his coach so much for what he stood for and the character, discipline and tools to win that he taught him throughout his career at Banks.

Knighton was a three-time All-State player at defensive tackle. In '74, his senior year, Knighton was selected as a high school All-American. Banks was also the number one team in the country then according to a national high school poll, the first time Knighton remembers that a poll was used to rank high school teams.

He was 6-0, 200 pounds and tougher than a jackhammer. Maybe one story best characterizes Knighton.

Freddie was in class one day when another student—angry with Knighton because Knighton had been going out with his girlfriend— walked up to Freddie. The night before, the other kid had made a threatening call to Knighton. "That girl was real pretty and I didn't think they were that serious, but he was a real jealous type. He ended up marrying the girl."

The other kid approached Knighton with a steel rod in his hands. "I looked up and the next thing I knew there was this pipe in front of my face."

The guy hit Knighton with the pipe across his mouth and then hit him over the head with it. Knighton, a little woozy, got out of his desk and put a form tackle on the other guy. "I hit him in the chest just like I did on the football field."

Freddie then grabbed the kid in a headlock and ran pulling the kid's head in his arms across the room. The other kids left their desks and cleared out as the teacher, Knighton recalls, "almost had a nervous breakdown." Knighton smashed the kid's head against the wall twice and knocked him out. The teacher told him frantically to never do that again in her classroom. Both Knighton and the other kid were sent to the Board of Education. The other student was suspended for 50 days for assaulting Knighton, but Knighton was allowed to return to school.

It was a testament to Freddie's toughness that he survived the blows. He had stitches above his mouth but played that Friday night.

Knighton displayed that kind of toughness on the football field where he was dedicated to his sport and would run through Fort Knox for his coach and his teammates.

Berry had tied Banks 14-14 in '72 and kept the Jets from a perfect season that year (the Jets won the state and went 12-0-1). In '73, Knighton and his teammates were driven to not let Berry win or even come close.

White had told his players all week about the Berry running backs who were anointing themselves Csonka and Kiick after Miami Dolphins' running backs Larry Csonka and Jim Kiick, two of the top running backs in the NFL who led the Dolphins to the Super Bowl in '72 and led them to the Super Bowl title in '73.

Knighton was particularly focused on not letting John Turpin—the Csonka part of the tandem—win the game for Berry. "I was not going to let him beat us," Knighton says. "If we were going to win we were going to have to stop him."

White had warned his players all week about "Csonka and Kiick". On an early Turpin run around the corner, Knighton faced off against a Berry lineman who'd play linebacker later at Alabama and another lineman who would become a heavyweight wrestler at Alabama. Knighton plowed through both of them and made a powerful hit on Turpin below the waist. Danny Beck, the Banks safety, hit him high. Turpin was knocked out of the game with a torn-up knee.

"It was a clean hit," White maintains to this day. "Freddie was not the type of kid to play dirty."

White found Turpin's number in Knighton's helmet after the game. Knighton says that he had a picture of Turpin on his wall at home all that week. Banks blasted Berry 35-6 on their way to another state championship that year. They finished '73 with a 13-0 record.

Knighton had a self-imposed determination and work ethic but his coach developed it even more. He has the utmost respect for his coach. "He taught me about respect. I wasn't afraid of him, I don't think he wanted that from any of the players. He just wanted you to give everything you had. One thing he didn't like was a lazy player."

Knighton saw in his coach a man who was an ethical person, always trying to do the right thing. "He was a religious man and talked to us about that. I try to do what's right and I learned a lot about that from him."

But Knighton does remember that his coach was a tough taskmaster.

"We'd practice at a boys' school in Roebuck and he'd have us practice from six to nine in the morning during two-a-days. He would give us ice instead of water because he thought we would cramp up drinking water. I remember we would run wind sprints 30 minutes after practice. That is a long time to run sprints. He'd run us till we dropped. But we were in the best condition of any team in the city. That's what made us so good."

Knighton says another thing that really stood out for him about his coach was his ability to get the team ready to play on Friday nights. "More than anything, I remembered how he motivated me. I will never forget those speeches he made before the game. Each one of them was different. He never had a speech that would carry over to the next week. It would always pertain to that team we were playing.

"He'd touch on the other team's good points. He'd also touch on their negatives but more on their good points. I really enjoyed his ability to get you out there to want to beat the other team. He would build that team up to where you'd say to yourself if I don't go out there and give it my all we're probably going to lose the game. He was like Coach Bryant. Coach Bryant always had something positive to say about the other team."

Knighton got a scholarship to play football at Alabama but quit after his second year.

"My parents had just gone through a divorce and my daddy was coming down to practice with his girlfriend and that really bothered me. I hated football at the time. That was a real regret for me that I didn't stay with it."

White went to Alabama as an assistant coach when Knighton started there in 1975.

"I was always curious how that was going to work out because Coach White would have to be under somebody. I never could picture him working under somebody but he stayed there five or six years ('75-'81)."

Knighton says his coach was highly focused on his duty at Banks. "He was serious. Coach White had a sense of humor about him but I never did look at him that way. He was focused on what he was doing, whether it was getting the practice field ready for the season or conducting a practice.

"Coaches nowadays don't put that kind of commitment into their job. In a job like that you've got to put as much into it as what your players do. He really put everything he had into it. I really believe that."

Freddie concedes that White had plenty of detractors, which came with his job.

"A lot of parents didn't like him because they thought he was too rough and he didn't put up with any of them. He had no patience for a whiner. He would just tell you what was on his mind. He didn't hold back any punches. That's why a lot of people didn't like him because he wasn't going to listen to their complaints. If you weren't going to do it his way, you could take your kid and go. That's the way it's supposed to be with a head coach. He was a leader and he ran the show. If you're going to get paid to do that job you need to do it the best way you know to do it. My daddy got sideways with him a couple of times but daddy still liked him."

White was controversial amongst his players too.

"We were teenagers and there was a lot of peer pressure to do things you shouldn't do. He'd know about it and he would confront you about it and want to know what was going on. I think we always had people who were not happy. He never liked hot dogs. Kids these days take their helmet off when they score touchdowns. Coach Bryant would roll over in his grave if he knew what was going on. Coach White wouldn't put up with that kind of thing. It was all about the team."

Knighton says that from '72-'74 when Banks reeled off 35 games in a row without a loss—the only tie coming against Berry 14-14 in '72—there were 12-13 players who received Division One scholarships. Banks was a dominant program, one revered and probably hated—like Hoover today—by other teams in the state, certainly in the city.

Freddie calls Hoover "a dynasty" but believes that Banks could win against Hoover, particularly the '73 team.

"Jeff [Rutledge] being as good as he was probably would have given us the edge over them. We had great receivers with a lot of speed and we were just as tough. They have more depth than we had but we were in such good condition that we could have beaten them that way."

That's a matter of debate and it's hard to compare. Both programs are true dynasties in Alabama football history.

Did Knighton have any doubt that Banks would win a game every time they went out there? With that 35-game streak it's hard to believe you would lose when you were so dominant.

"There were doubts, yes," the high school All-American recalls. "When we played Woodlawn in '74 and earlier. West End was always a tough game."

Knighton notes that White was more engaged than Bryant, his college coach, as far as conducting practice.

"Coach White knew everything about what was going on out there. Coach Bryant would stay in his tower and come down when he thought something was not going right on the field.

"We had the best weight room in the city. Coach White would let people who didn't play use it. He took a lot of pride in that facility."

White, his coaches, players and their parents—who had the most to do with it—built the weight house at Banks from the ground up in the late '60s. White was, and still is, a firm believer in "the steel" as he calls it.

Knighton, when asked who was the best football coach he played for, says there is no doubt it was White.

"He was the best coach I ever had. He knew football. He knew offense and he perfected the Veer."

The Veer allowed Gary and Jeff Rutledge to run the triple option; they could give to the fullback, fake it to him and run around the corner, pitch to the tailback or throw it. Actually four options.

"He knew how to run plays and read defenses and he knew how to explain it to you," Freddie explains. "He could sit in his office and draw plays up all day."

White was the ultimate tough, hard-nosed football coach, but Knighton says there was a soft side to him.

"He never cussed at you or hit you. He yelled but he never cussed. I respected that. He did what he thought was best for you.

"He did have a soft side though he didn't show it much at the time. But every time I've seen him since, he gives me a big old hug. He's kind of mellowed out through the years. He really cared about his players. I love the man, I really do."

Knighton specifically remembers "Shorty White Day" at Banks, a reunion of players and boosters from the glory years.

"Coach White was giving a speech saying how much he enjoyed the kids and how special we were to him. I was walking up the steps and he said, 'here comes one of them now.' I felt like crying."

For Knighton, despite a tough, determined and driven personality, White was a man who truly cared about his players and taught them the value of being a good person, working hard and displaying integrity at all times. If you did that for White, you were his type of guy.

All of White's assistants were committed to his mentality. Dyer Carlisle coached with Shorty White at Banks from '73-'74 then was the head coach at Banks when White left for Alabama; the team went 15-15 in three years. He remembers White's intense focus on getting the job done no matter what other people said.

Carlisle was the defensive coordinator for White when Banks won the state in '73, and went 9-2 in '74. Banks only allowed 122 points in

13 games in '73 (9.4 ppg.) and 87 points in '74 in 11 games (7.9). Carlisle, like many others who coached under White, agrees that White taught him what it took to be a head coach.

"In '73, we beat Grissom for the state championship and in '74, Jeff broke his ankle the last game of the season against West End. Homewood got a gift, winning the state championship that year. We were clearly the best team in the state and Woodlawn was the second best team."

Woodlawn didn't make the playoffs that year as far fewer teams qualified for the playoffs—there were three rounds of playoffs in the postseason. Carlisle went 2-8 his first year as head coach at Banks. He lost 21 starters off the '74 team and his only returning starter, Frankie Gunnels, strained his abdomen and missed significant playing time. His last year at Banks, Dyer was 7-3.

Dyer remembers that White was "really good to me." Carlisle was 23 years old when he started for White. He coached with Bob Finley while he was a student at Samford. He coached at West End out of college for Bob Haggard in 1971. Haggard took West End to the playoffs, where they lost to eventual state champion Decatur. Four players off that West End team went to Auburn to play. Haggard went to Haleyville and Carlisle followed him for one year, then White hired him at Banks when Robert Higginbotham took the Mountain Brook head coaching job.

"He was a great tactician," Carlisle says of White. "Particularly offensively. He was really ahead of his time. It's a travesty he's not been elected to the Hall of Fame."

Carlisle likens White to Rush Propst of Hoover in his supreme confidence to get the job done. "He's a modern-day Shorty White. Shorty didn't endear himself to many other coaches. A lot of it had to do with him beating them so many times."

Dyer calls White "a master strategist. He was tremendously dedicated. He loved football and spent a lot of time on it. It was pretty much his life."

Carlisle, as many others, echoed that the weight room was so nice and so ahead of its time at Banks that college football players would work out in it. It would not be unusual to see Johnny Musso or Pat Sullivan working out at Banks. "There were SEC players working out in the Banks weight room. It was pretty neat."

Dyer also says that White was the strictest disciplinarian you could find when it came to appearance and conduct. Carlisle remembers White and Joe Shaw, one of his '73 standouts, always locking horns on the length of Shaw's locks. White called him out from practice and told him to get to the barbershop.

"Joe replied that he went to the barbershop yesterday which was a Wednesday and it was closed. Coach said you never would know when the barbershop was open or closed. He would never hold back from calling out players."

Dyer remembers Bear Bryant coming to a Banks game to look at Rutledge among others and complimenting White and the other coaches after the game by saying, "Banks is the finest-coached high school team I have seen in a long time."

Carlisle knows White had some options. The University of Wyoming head coaching position was a possibility at one time in the '60s but never materialized. White would have gone there. Ole Miss wanted White after the '74 season, according to Carlisle, as a package deal with Jeff Rutledge. But Bryant wanted White as a coach because he had high regard for White's coaching ability.

"Shorty was like Rush Propst in that he would have traded an arm and a leg to get into college coaching."

White finally did in 1975 at Alabama.

Carlisle says that White was driven to excel.

"He was not an easy person to play for or to work for, but I loved the guy. I learned so much from him."

And Carlisle gives June White credit.

"She's a story in herself for putting up with him and raising a fine family. You won't find a lot of people who are middle of the road on Coach White. I thought a lot of him. There were people who disliked him—mostly his opponents."

CHAPTER 13
35-Game Streak Snapped (1974)

White entered the '74 season believing this was the most talented team he had coached in his tenure at Banks High School. With All-American Jeff Rutledge behind center, a cast of all-star skill players including Jerry Murphree, Jerry McDonald and Bob Grefseng and a defense led by enforcer Freddie Knighton, White thought the only roadblock keeping this team from winning the state title would be injuries.

The team breezed through the first eight games of the season allowing only 33 points and scoring 336. The Jets beat Hayes 71-0, Ramsay 42-0, Berry 28-7 and rival Huffman 35-0. White was cautiously optimistic. The key to his team's success was not only their talent, but their conditioning. White put his players through rigorous, intense practices. And he didn't leave any stone unturned. He would work on the kicking game on Monday, working on punt coverage and kickoff coverage. Then he would focus on the offense and the defense. On Tuesday he would proceed after warm-ups (which the team started out with every practice) to punt return, kickoff return and field goals, then focus on defense first, then offense.

"Defense keeps you from losing, so it's the most important thing," White says. "Offense can win you games but defense keeps you in the game and ultimately wins it for you. We stressed the kicking game a lot too."

On Wednesday, White would work on areas of the kicking game that needed to be shored up and of course go over offense and defense. Thursday would be a walk-through, going over assignments for the games particularly in the kicking game.

And there was always conditioning in the last 15-20 minutes of practice. White prided himself on having the best-conditioned football players in the state.

"I told my kids before games that nobody has outworked you, and you are in better shape than anybody else," he says. "Games were fun. I just said something positive to them before the games. I had done all my yelling during the week."

White had been a master at conditioning since learning that skill from the military. He had had such a depressing experience at Auburn in football, but he proved himself as a football player in the military.

"Auburn was the first time I had experienced failure as an athlete," he admits. "I was always practicing hard. I could knock anybody on their tail. I was practicing in the secondary one time and a guy kept trying to cut block me and take my knees out. I told Coach [Gene] Lorendo that the next time he did that, I was going to hurt him. When he came back at me I put my elbow in his jaw and knocked him out. I told Coach Lorendo, 'I told you I was going to do that.' He started laughing like crazy."

White used that frustrating experience at Auburn as a motivator in coaching. He was going to succeed and he was going to do it his way. He stayed true to his ways and his methods led to many successful Friday nights.

Banks's ninth game in '74 was against rugged rival Woodlawn. The game was at Legion Field, both teams were undefeated (Banks was 8-0 and Woodlawn was 9-0) and both teams featured an offensive All-American, Banks's Rutledge and Woodlawn's superior running back Tony Nathan. Freddie Knighton on defense for Banks was an All-American too. There was a buzz throughout the city as the game approached.

White expected a huge turnout for the game. He told the Legion Field authorities that they would need to open the side gates to let all the people into the stadium. White anticipated the largest crowd in high school history since a Legion Field game he starred in, the 1950 Phillips-Ramsay game that drew 38,000 fans.

White says he was nervous all week.

"They were very good, they were ahead of us physically, not in determination and work ethic but just in their size and their abilities."

Forty-two thousand people showed up for the game. As White had predicted there were many more trying to get in, but because only one gate was opened, Birmingham Police Chief Connie Pitts estimated that 20,000 fans turned around and went home.

Banks dominated the game. Nathan scored a late touchdown to make the final margin 18-7. White and his players were now 9-0 heading into the last game of the season but the Woodlawn battle was a fiercely contested game and took its toll on White's team.

White says his team was flat in the West End game. White's fear of injuries crippling his thin team came to pass : when Rutledge was rolling out to pass in the first quarter, he was tackled and broke his ankle.

"When you've lost your number one player and a player of that caliber it's demoralizing. It was very, very difficult after that happened."

White sent son Gary in the game and Banks did score a lot of points but lost to West End 35-27. It was the end of a 35-game streak without a loss.

"It was depressing, I was worn out, so were my players."

The next week, the first round of the playoffs against Homewood, Gary White got the flu and missed the first three days of practice. White told his son that he would have to practice Thursday if he was going to play in the game.

Gary practiced Thursday and played. Though Gary gave a valiant effort, without Rutledge the offense wasn't the same. Banks had one great opportunity to seize momentum. White called a lateral to his flanker who was to throw a pass down field to the tight end. Banks was deep in its own territory. The tight end was wide open.

"If that play had worked we could have won the game," Coach White remembers.

But the flanker dropped the ball attempting to pass, Homewood recovered the fumble and took it in for their only touchdown of the game.

"That flanker was so down, bless his heart."

Homewood kicked two field goals and won the game 12-0.

The losses at the end of the season stung but didn't take away from what all that senior class had accomplished. Two state championships, 35 games without a loss and what in all probability would have been a third title had Rutledge not gone down against West End.

And White was so proud of what his players accomplished off the field. Rutledge was president of the class and Mr. Football in the state of Alabama. Bob Grefseng and Rutledge along with Randy Dupre were in the National Honor Society. Jerry Murphree, who made one of the greatest runs White ever saw his junior year, when he ran through three defenders, keeping his balance with one hand and diving into the end zone in a playoff game, was the B team president of the Athletic Club. Grefseng was the vice president, Rutledge was the chaplain and the sergeant of arms was none other than Freddie Knighton.

There was a great tribute to Rutledge as Mr. Banks. The tribute described his accomplishments as a person and what a true friend he was to fellow students.

They were great years and a special class for White.

"The buildings at the school were not that great, but the kids, they were a class act."

After the class of '75 graduation, White accepted a job as assistant football coach at the University of Alabama where he coached under Bear Bryant and was part of a staff behind the scenes of national championships in 1978 and 1979. Two of the players on the '78 team were Jeff Rutledge and Tony Nathan, two stars who were part of the greatest game in Alabama high school football history.

White enjoyed his Alabama years but nothing has replaced the memories at one special place as a coach who made it a special experience for the players under his watch. George "Shorty" White forever left his mark in Alabama high school football history. It's a legacy that should never be forgotten.

CHAPTER 14
"Bear" Calls (1975-1977)

George "Shorty" White had taken Banks High School to the pinnacle of high school football in the state of Alabama. Three state championships, one in '65 and two in a row in '72 and '73—along with a '74 team that would surely have won one had it not been for an injury to All-American quarterback Jeff Rutledge in the last game of the regular season—earned him the right to decide what he wanted to do in the future in the coaching business. He probably could have gotten any high school coaching position he wanted in Alabama, but he wanted to accomplish something on a higher level, make more money and give his three children a chance at a fine college education.

Bear Bryant gave him that opportunity in January of '75. Bryant called White to come down to Tuscaloosa and talk to him at a restaurant outside of town. White had the flu and didn't feel like going but the attractiveness of coaching in Tuscaloosa for Bryant was too much for White to resist.

White met Bryant at the restaurant to talk and there were many people coming up to the table to talk to Bryant. Bear told White that they needed to talk in his car. White says that he sat with him in Bryant's car with the windows rolled up—it was cold outside—while Bryant was smoking Chesterfields. White, already having trouble breathing, had to crack the window to get some air. White and Bryant agreed on a position at Alabama. White would coach running backs. When White got out of the car, he remembers Bryant barking, "Roll up the damn window!"

White had accomplished so much at Banks against some of the best competition in the state in the 60's and 70's in the Birmingham area. Ramsay, Woodlawn, Ensley, West End some years and Jones Valley some years presented a huge challenge for a coach to prepare for. Those teams were tough, solid and very well coached. And White beat them consistently.

From '75-'80, White was part of an Alabama staff that helped the Tide go 64-8, win every bowl game they played in, and win two national championships in '78 and '79. Alabama never lost to Auburn in those years, never lost to Tennessee either. White recruited fourteen players on the '79 national championship team.

White said there was not a lot of pressure from Bryant though much was expected. The pressure was internal. The staff was filled with great coaches and they were committed to doing whatever it took to succeed. White found out one year that Bryant was going to have to cut his staff because there were NCAA rules restricting the number of coaches a program was allowed to have. White kept his job and was relieved.

White brought his expertise in weight training to the university and was instrumental in vastly upgrading the weight training for the Alabama football team.

White was the running backs coach, and he coached some fine players. He taught them solid blocking and running techniques. He would grade his running backs every week, as all the coaches did, to let them know how they stood. Willie Shelby, one of the most exciting running backs to ever put on an Alabama uniform, challenged White on his grade one week.

"I tried to be as fair with them as I could without giving them credit for what they didn't accomplish," White shrugs.

White told Shelby to come over to his office after class, and they would review the film of the game. Shelby and White went over the game and Shelby gave himself a lower grade than White had!

"He never challenged me again," White says. "Nobody else did."

White was a stickler for devastating blocking technique and he trained some of the best blockers in the SEC. Shelby made one of "the prettiest load blocks at Tennessee I've ever seen. He hit the guy's outside knee and rose up to make it a legal block and wiped him out."

The other block White taught was Bryant's Junction Block, made famous at Texas A&M when Bryant coached there and had his famous Junction Boys outfit, that included Gene Stallings and 30 or so other players, who survived a brutal preseason boot camp and went on to win the Southwest Conference title the next year. The back would step to the outside foot of the defensive end, stay down low and go through him. This block could neutralize a linebacker also. White said his players got pretty good at both blocks.

White had incredible success at Tuscaloosa but it didn't start off that way. The first game of the '75 season was against Missouri and the

Tide coaching staff was totally caught off guard with the defense that the Tigers ran. The coaches worked on what Missouri had been previously running, a standard 4-3 or a 5-2, but Missouri came out in an 8-gap defense with eight guys on the line and three players deep. Alabama couldn't read anything on that defense and Alabama's Wishbone offense was totally shut down. Missouri won the game 20-7. "We learned a lot from that," White says. "We started working against multiple defensive fronts in practice. It could have been a blessing."

White and Bill Oliver had scouted the Clemson Tigers the Saturday before—Clemson was the second game of the season—and saw that Clemson took a lot of time getting their punts off. Oliver had put a stopwatch on Clemson and saw that they were slow. White and Oliver wrote on the report to defensive coordinator Ken Donahue that they could block a punt.

"They punted from their own five-yard line and boom! We blocked it," White recalls with gusto. "It turned into a slaughter."

The Tide won that game 56-0 and then put together an outstanding season, winning their next 10 straight to finish 11-1. They beat Tennessee 30-7, Auburn 28-0 and Penn State in the Sugar Bowl 13-6.

White remembers quarterback Robert Fraley as a "great young guy." Fraley went on to become a highly accomplished agent in sports. He tragically died in the plane crash that killed PGA golfer Payne Stewart, who had just recently won the U.S. Open in 1999 at Pinehurst, North Carolina.

One time late in a Vanderbilt game, White told Fraley, a backup to Richard Todd, to fake the belly play to the fullback, fake the hand off to the left halfback, and keep the ball and run it. Fraley went over 50 yards for a touchdown. "He hugged my neck," White says. "He had wanted to score." Fraley was from Nashville.

But the Crimson Tide lost some "sickening games" to Notre Dame. Alabama lost twice to the Fighting Irish when White was there.

In the '76 game at South Bend, the Tide lost a heartbreaker, 21-18.

In the '80 game at Legion Field, the entire backfield was injured and Bryant had to start freshman Walter Lewis at quarterback and Linnie Patrick, an outstanding player in high school but only a freshman, at fullback. He was undersized, as he was normally a halfback. The Tide lost that game to Notre Dame 7-0.

White remembers so many outstanding players at the University during his tenure. He calls Dwight Stephenson, who played center from '77-'79, "something special."

"I say that because of his work ethic. He went 100 percent. He didn't know 99 or 95 percent. In the huddle he would talk to himself. He would have that serious look on his face during scrimmages. If we had a drill he would go for all the marbles. He was the most competitive guy I've ever been around. The other one was Ozzie Newsome."

Stephenson went on to have a highly successful pro career with the Miami Dolphins.

Newsome, an All-Pro at Cleveland in the NFL, played for the Tide from '74-'77. "Ozzie had character," White says. "He could play tight end or split end. He was a big guy who could run. He could block, he could do it all."

Jim Bunch was an offensive lineman for Alabama from '76-'79, not very big, about 225 or 230 pounds but "he would get off the ball and mash you. He was outstanding."

White also remembers David Hannah, who played at Alabama from '75-'79, one of the famous Hannah brothers. Older brother John played from '70-'72. He was an All-American and one of the greatest offensive linemen in NFL history, playing for the New England Patriots. Charles—another older brother—played for the Tide from '74-'76. "All the Hannahs were good. They just had size and talent."

David Hannah is now helping with the Briarwood Christian offensive line and White told him in 2006 that "he had made a difference in the football program."

Another player White says stood out to him was linebacker Woodrow Lowe, who played from '72-'75. "That dude was good. He was a senior my first year there."

White also points to Bob Baumhower ('74-'76), Marty Lyons ('77-'78) and Steve Whitman, "my favorite fullback," ('77-'79) as standouts.

Lyons is famous for informing Penn State quarterback Chuck Fusina that "you better pass" when Penn State had the ball on the Alabama one, fourth and goal, time running down, in the national championship 1979 Sugar Bowl. Penn State decided to run it, Lyons and Barry Krauss stuffed Mike Guman, and Alabama won its fifth national championship under Bear Bryant. They won their sixth under Bear in the 1980 Sugar Bowl, a 24-9 win over Arkansas.

White says that the '78 and '79 teams were special because the majority of the players remain good people later in life. It was a special time in Tuscaloosa.

White remembers the bowl trips as always special. It was the one time the wives could travel with the coaches on road trips.

Shorty remembers a bowl trip to New Orleans when the coaches went to an oyster bar and ordered a huge quantity of raw oysters. Bobby Marks out-ate all the coaches. Marks coached Darryl, White's son, at wide receiver; Marks was a good coach and a fine person, in Shorty's estimation.

White says it was as if he and the team lived in New Orleans in early January as Alabama went to the Sugar Bowl four times while he was there. They also went to the Liberty Bowl and the Cotton Bowl. In the '76 Sugar Bowl, UCLA was a big favorite over the Tide, but Ken Donahue had watched the Bruins on film and noticed that one of the offensive linemen tipped off when the offense was going to pass. The Tide destroyed the Bruins 36-6. "They didn't have a prayer," White recalls.

Shorty says that Donahue, who coached at Alabama from '64-'84, was a master at breaking down offenses. "I loved him. I roomed with him on the road. He would find any little advantage to give us an edge. He was the best I've ever seen. He was also quite a guy. The other coaches wouldn't want to room with him on the road because he would stay up so late watching film on the projector in the hotel room. He'd be at work at 5:45. There wasn't anybody as committed as Ken Donahue. I really miss him."

White says that work was year-round. After the season, there was off-season work and recruiting, then getting ready for spring training. After spring, maybe time to take a two-week vacation, but summers were devoted to scouting different teams for the next season. The coaches had to make reports off the film they watched of the upcoming season's opponents. But White loved it. He was passionate.

"I was blessed and fortunate to be at the University of Alabama. That era couldn't get any better."

In '77 White was succeeding as an assistant coach at Alabama, working long hours trying to help the program win more football games.

The Tide went 12-1 in '77 with their only loss coming to Nebraska in Lincoln, 31-24. White had responsibility for preparing the team for the Louisville and Georgia games. Alabama beat Georgia 18-10 and smacked Louisville 55-6. Each assistant was responsible for preparing the team for two games during the season along with their on-field coaching responsibilities. White broke down all the games from the year before of the opponent he was scouting.

One of the memorable games from '77 was the victory over Southern Cal in Los Angeles, 21-20. "They had great skill players; anytime you play a team like Southern Cal, Nebraska or Ohio State and you beat them, it's quite an accomplishment." 'Bama also beat Miami that year

36-0. "They were so cocky, mouthing off in the press about how they were going to beat us. They ran their mouths too much. The team took 'em to the cleaners."

Alabama's SEC wins were over Georgia, Ole Miss (34-13), Vandy (24-12), Tennessee (24-10), Mississippi State (37-7), LSU (24-3) and Auburn (48-21).

The Tide then faced an Ohio State team that was very hard-nosed in the Sugar Bowl. Alabama beat them 35-6 behind Jeff Rutledge and Tony Nathan. The '77 season set the stage for two national championships in '78 and '79.

White says he had a good relationship with most of the running backs who played for him. Three of his favorites were Steve Whitman, Lou Ikner and Major Ogilvie.

"It was hard to really enjoy a season until it was over. 1977 was not any different from any other season. You'd go from season to season, spring training to spring training."

White says that all bowl games were a thrill for June and the other coaches' wives.

"They had a ball. They had places to go and see and ate at great restaurants. We were working a lot of the time."

One of White's favorite stories involves Shorty playing golf in the SEC coaches' meeting with other assistant coaches throughout the conference. It was played at the Birmingham Country Club. He won the award for what he thinks was Worst Golfer Out There. After the tournament, he and defensive coordinator Ken Donahue went to Florida on a scouting trip. When he got home at three in the morning June and the kids were waiting up for him. He had received a Lincoln Versailles as a gift for the golf tournament. He got to drive it for a year. "There were some jealous assistant coaches," he crows.

White says the staff that Bear Bryant had assembled at Alabama was "outstanding—a great group and dedicated to what they were doing." The coordinators were Ken Donahue and Mal Moore.

White says that Rutledge was coming into his own his junior year in Tuscaloosa and could have really flourished in a system emphasizing the passing game. Jeff still put a lot of wins on the scoreboard for his team.

"His talent did not fit in the Wishbone. How he did as well as he did is remarkable. He fit the mold of a modern-day quarterback. If we had stressed a passing game, he would have stood out with the best of all Alabama quarterbacks. Breaking records, completions, and yardage are not nearly as important as points on the scoreboard."

The Crimson Tide was legendary for their overstocked backfield and one of White's favorite runners was James Taylor. Taylor ran wild as an All-State running back at Citronelle High School where, in his senior season (the only season he played) he gained almost 2,000 yards and scored 16 touchdowns. He was a prized recruit and signed with the University as just another one of the All-Star running backs hoarded by Coach Bryant.

Taylor was a key player his senior year on a 'Bama team that went 11-1 in '75, losing its first game to Missouri then reeling off 11 wins capped by a 13-6 Sugar Bowl victory over Penn State (the first year the Sugar Bowl was played in the Superdome). Taylor played with Willie Shelby, Calvin Culliver, Randy Billingsley, Mike Stock, Duffey Boles, Johnny Davis and Tony Nathan, legends in the Wishbone offense. Taylor believes that the Crimson Tide was the best team in the nation at the end of the '75-'76 season and also believes that the starting nine (three sets of running backs in the rotation) could have started for any team in the SEC.

Coach White's first year was '75, Taylor's senior season. Taylor says that he and White forged a tremendous friendship that he will never forget.

"He was just an open, honest guy. When I had a problem I felt like I could go to him. He was the same on the field as he was off the field. He was just a good friend."

Taylor reiterates what many of White's Banks players say and that is, White was demanding of his players and expected perfection. But Taylor also says that White was dedicated to his players and only wanted them to be the best they could be.

"He didn't hold anything back, he would fuss at you like any boss would fuss at somebody who works for him, but he didn't play favorites. Sometimes you get coaches who play the same player every week. Coach White was not like that."

James lost his dad when he was nine years old and worked a farm running a tractor or herding cattle; he was used to hard work. He went out for football on a dare and excelled at it at Citronelle High. But in high school, he never had to block and under Coach Bryant that was mandatory.

"I was used to carrying the ball 30 times a game but in college it was probably four times a game. We had to take on big defensive ends and linebackers or sometimes defensive backs or safeties when we ran the option. I remember blocking Steve Niehaus of Notre Dame who weighed about 300 pounds and had legs as big as tree trunks. It was like going against John Hannah. They both would knock you off like you were a fly. It didn't take a rocket scientist to know who was going to win that battle. But we had a lot of success with the Wishbone. I wish it was being played today."

Taylor says that White was passionate about the game and conveyed that passion to his running backs.

"He didn't seem to get very emotional about a lot of things, but he was emotional about playing football. That vein would stick out of his neck and his face would get red. He'd be ready to go."

James Taylor is adamant that White could have been a very successful college coach if he had gotten the opportunity.

"He believed in giving 110 percent every time out. He wanted his players to play wide open. I personally think I caught Coach White at a time when he was in transition from being a head coach and running his own show at Banks High School. I wish I could have played for him when he was a head coach. He was hard-headed. I've got my own business and most people who work for me say I'm hard-headed. I think most bosses are. I really believe he could have gotten a Division II job and gone from there and really excelled. He was a great guy. The thing I liked most about him is that he was the same person off the field as he was on the field."

CHAPTER 15
Fitted For Rings (1978-1979)

Major Ogilvie was a winner in high school and a winner in college. He was the heart and soul of the Mountain Brook High School teams that won state championships in '75 and '76 under Shorty White protégé Robert Higginbotham, a very fine coach who believed in discipline and toughness. Ogilvie exhibited those characteristics throughout his high school career as a running back and brought them down to Tuscaloosa. Ogilvie was a key player on national championship teams at Alabama in '78 and '79. Major Ogilvie was a winner—he holds an NCAA record, scoring at least one touchdown in each of four bowl games. Injury prevented this gifted back with a nose for the end zone from pursuing an NFL career.

Major remembers White as an excellent teacher and a natural leader.

"He's an interesting guy and he accomplished a lot of great things," Ogilvie says. "He was a great teacher, very good with details. He helped me tremendously with my footwork to give me the best chance to make a play."

Ogilvie says that White was teaching what Coach Bryant wanted taught.

"When you played running back for Coach Bryant you had to block and it all started with your footwork. And there were certain blocks that I had no idea how to do. I did, but I didn't understand how important the footwork was. Shorty taught me to keep my right foot planted and explode with my left foot. Coach White was great with the details."

Ogilvie says that White is also a master at teaching quarterback play. Ogilvie's son, Morgan, is a standout quarterback at Mountain Brook High School and worked under White one day.

"He has tremendous knowledge of the skills and the little

techniques it takes to be a successful quarterback. He's very good at teaching those things.

"Another thing is Coach White made it fun for us. Our practices at Alabama were long—they were just forever. Coach White kept it fun. He's got a little different outlook on things and I mean that in a positive way. When we used to come through the tunnel and get ready for practice— we would be stretching—Coach White would sing to us. He'd sing, 'If I die in the combat zone, put me in a box and ship me home. Lay my hand across my chest, and tell my girl I did my best.' Our practices were really hard and it was not like we were going off to war but it wasn't far from it either. He believed in people and he was very kind and supportive of me when I was at the University. I'll always be grateful to him."

Ogilvie not only learned how to improve his blocking but he also learned how to run with the football in a very effective way from White. It was all basic and made a lot of sense.

"One thing you learned real quick is you've got to go north and south. There isn't much in college football going east and west. Coach White pointed me north and said don't think about going any other directions. Today some teams go east and west and they're the wannabes but the good teams still go north and south."

Major says it was just a tough, military-style training that White and Coach Bryant took to the football field that made Bryant's teams better than their opponents.

"That's why we won my junior year. We were not as talented; we were just mentally and physically tougher. It doesn't make sense to go through all that work and go out and lose. If you look back on it, half the teams we played had more skill, more talent than we had at Alabama, but we were just tougher than our opponents. My junior year at Mountain Brook we won because we were tougher than anybody. We had to pay the price the same way we did at Alabama and we won a lot of games because we were tougher than the other team."

To Major, White was his own man, and that while he was a dedicated assistant coach he was in an unusual position on the staff.

"He was probably the only coach at Alabama who did not play for Coach Bryant. I don't recall another coach on the staff who hadn't played for him. I thought that was interesting."

Another All-American running back for the Crimson Tide, Tony Nathan was perhaps Coach White's most talented opponent in high school. Nathan was an All-American running back for Woodlawn High School, which had many hard-fought wars with Banks, one particularly in November of '74 in the storied game at Legion Field.

Nathan signed with Alabama and played for Bear Bryant and Shorty White from '75-'78 when White was the running backs coach in Tuscaloosa. Nathan, now the running backs coach for the Baltimore Ravens, remembers White as a coach who was as serious and dedicated to his job as Tony was about being the best running back he could be. Nathan was a key player on the '78 national championship team at Alabama that defeated the Penn State Nittany Lions 14-7 in the '79 Sugar Bowl.

Nathan, a reflective man, remembers the Banks-Woodlawn rivalry as intense and high-spirited. It was a bitter rivalry with both teams trying to beat the other physically as well as on the scoreboard. Emotions were sky high for the games.

"We didn't get along too well," Nathan says in an understated tone. "I didn't really know Coach White in high school. I heard Jeff Rutledge talk about him. At Alabama he was a high-spirited individual."

Rutledge and Nathan were the major players featured on the front of *The Birmingham News* the day of the Banks-Woodlawn game in 1974. Banks won a hard-fought, intense game, 18-7. White is always quick to say that his team never recovered from that game physically the rest of the season, as they lost to West End the following week, in the last game of the season, ending a 35-game streak of games without a loss. Banks then lost to eventual state champion Homewood in the first round of the playoffs. Three of the Banks defensive starters were knocked out for the rest of the season after the Woodlawn game.

"It was like the Alabama-Auburn rivalry," Nathan says of the Banks-Woodlawn game. "Just on a smaller level. We didn't beat them while I was there, which was a thorn in my side. Coach (Tandy) Geralds respected him. Shorty was doing a great job up there at Banks."

But Nathan remembers White primarily as an excellent teacher on the football field at Alabama.

"He was not overbearing like I had heard he was in high school. He pushed you to do what you needed to do in order to get the job done."

Nathan gained a lot of insight which he uses today in his coaching career from playing under White and Bear Bryant.

"I learned that if I ever wanted to be a coach I had to be thorough in planning and make sure that people understood what I was trying to accomplish. As a player I became a student of the game. What I learned from Coach White was how to communicate to the players what we were responsible for. He got his point across."

White was known as a tough, hard-nosed taskmaster and Nathan says that came with the profession of coaching in those times.

"Back in that day every coach was that way to a degree. Shorty pushed you to your limit so you could find out what your limits were. But that was part of the program. If you were in that program you worked hard, period, regardless, if you wanted to play."

Nathan recalls that White was a reflection of Nathan's head coach at Alabama.

"He was just reiterating what Coach Bryant stood for and what he wanted done. He was just confirming how hard we needed to work. His job was to make us the best players we could be at the time."

Tony remembers vividly the Banks game in 1974. He was ready to play in front of an electric audience of 42,000 at Legion Field in one of the most famous, if not the most famous game in Alabama high school football history.

"It was nothing like I've ever experienced before in my life. People couldn't get in the stadium. I had never seen a crowd that big for a high school game. We were sitting around waiting to play the game at 7:30 and we ended up playing at 8:30 or a quarter till nine. That's a long time to sit around and wait. They were a better football team that night."

Nathan remembers racial tensions did not prevail among football players during a highly charged time in the early '70s. Football was a bonding experience far away from racial problems in everyday life.

"The athletes got along. We suffered the pain together. You understood and appreciated the man next to you if he was doing what he was supposed to be doing. It was altogether different."

Nathan says that racism was a factor in those times in Birmingham but it was not encouraged by people who were educated, rather by people who weren't.

"I grew to understand that hatred most of the time comes from ignorance. It was from not knowing the other side and judging people wrongly. I must say that I was guilty of it to a certain degree. I learned from my parents that that was not the way to be. They didn't raise me that way. We had fights, stuff like that. I learned that you can't judge people by the color of their skin. It opened my mind and my heart about a lot of things."

The high school All-American had heard some stories about White, that he was not open-minded when it came to race but learned at Alabama that that was not true.

"I had heard some horror stories about him and I didn't know that man from Adam when he was at Banks. When I played for him he was not that way. He gave everybody an opportunity. He was fair. He expected a lot from you but he would not judge you by race."

Tony says the same about Coach Bryant.

"I didn't think Coach Bryant was that type of man. He didn't want to be associated with anybody who was like that. In other places where I was recruited, I'm not going to kiss and tell, you saw it and heard it, but not with Coach Bryant."

Nathan not only excelled on the prep level and on the college level but he was also an outstanding professional football player. He played on two Super Bowl teams with Don Shula's Miami Dolphins. He went to the Super Bowl in 1983 when the Dolphins played the Washington Redskins and in 1985 when the Dolphins played the San Francisco 49ers.

"I didn't get a ring and I had two opportunities to do so. That was the most disappointing thing about it. I wish I could have gotten one, but there are a lot of people in this business who don't get a chance to go to the Super Bowl and I got a chance to play in two. I was blessed in that respect."

Nathan says that his football career was successful because of the way he was taught how to work and achieve and to respect his career goals.

"It was hard work, dedication to your profession and you had to have respect for the man across the way from you."

Nathan noticed the same things about Bryant and Shula. They were the ultimate coaches.

"They both demanded a lot from you. They stressed giving it your all and if you didn't, you had every chance to cheat yourself and your teammates. They both believed in leaving it on the field and saving nothing.

"Coach Shula was more vocal than Coach Bryant. Coach Bryant was a man of few words but when he would speak everybody would listen. They were almost the same in that they were disciplinarians. They both knew their craft and they were ahead of their time in the game. They made the game basically what it is today."

Tony had a little trepidation playing the game at first but hung in there assisted by a push from his parents. He couldn't be happier with that decision.

"I loved it. I did it at first because my friends were playing. When they decided they didn't want to play my sophomore year in high school, I didn't want to play. But my mom said I wasn't going to be the first Nathan to quit. She made me go back and I thank her for it every day."

Nathan is convinced that he's learned more about the game at each level he's competed at.

"I enjoyed my high school years. At the college level you get to the point where you think you know everything and you learn that you don't know half of what you thought you knew. Then you learn some more in the pros. It becomes a chess game with the guy across the way from you trying to make the right moves at the right time. As a coach, you learn how to attack people and you learn how to deal with a young man with money. There is always something to learn from the game."

Nathan says his experience playing for Coach White at Alabama was fulfilling and educational as he grew in football and in life.

"He was a serious individual. He was just like Coach Bryant. He was respectful. Coach White would reach out to a kid and help a kid."

CHAPTER 16
Two More Bowls (1980-1981)

Shorty White has many fond memories of his tenure at Alabama. He met some of the best coaches and players in the business and had a favorable impression of all of them.

Woody Hayes was known for his hard-nosed, gruff demeanor and is remembered mostly for hitting a Clemson player in the 1982 Gator Bowl after the Clemson player intercepted an Ohio State pass. He was fired immediately after that incident.

But White says that Hayes was not the man who was portrayed on television. He was an old school football coach who would push his assistants aside when he didn't agree with what they were teaching and he was extremely demanding of his players, both mentally and physically like Bryant. But White remembers him as a pleasant, personable man.

White went up to Ohio State with fellow assistants Bobby Marks, Dee Powell and Ken Donahue to talk to Hayes and his coaches and get their feedback on teaching the game.

"He was not anything like he was made out to be in the Clemson game," White says. "He was a nice guy. He was getting ready to take all his secretaries out to lunch. He was really fun to be around. He was interesting and nice to me. He acted like he had known me forever. He was old school tough. He believed in defense and the running game. He was a blocking and tackling coach. He reminded me of Patton. He looked at football like it was war. Patton was a historian on the battlefield. He would go to battle, look around and say he had been there before. He was talking about a battle fought 2000 years before. Woody Hayes treated his football players like ground troops. He was a holy terror on the football field, pushing his coordinators out of the way. He would have a ramp ready for his players to run up and down before practice started. He would run them until they got tired. Off the field he was nice and polite. But that guy hated to lose. He was a competitor."

White also met Penn State Coach Joe Paterno when White was in charge of a coaching clinic in Tuscaloosa that Bryant sponsored for high school coaches. Paterno was known around the country as a first-class person and White says that he was just that.

"Coach Bryant respected him. I went to pick him up at the airport. Coming back from the airport he was very cordial and didn't talk to me like he was up here and I was down there. He was a nice, friendly guy. I watched him on the sidelines though and he was something. He saw something he didn't like and he would get stirred up and would jump down a referee's throat. But he was really a gentleman."

White also remembers Lee Roy Jordan, one of the best linebackers to ever suit up for the Crimson Tide and one of Bryant's personal favorites. Jordan also had an outstanding career as middle linebacker for the Dallas Cowboys; he was a major player on the 1972 Super Bowl Championship team.

"He had just retired and he was talking about the 4-3 defense that they had run in Dallas. He covered the techniques and alignments and was very knowledgeable. He didn't get into coaching because he saw he could make more money in buying land. He was very successful in business. He wins every day of his life. I've seen him recently and he's walking with a cane. He's had two knee replacements. The running backs feared him at Alabama. He would strike you like a snake. He was like Musso. They would strike you like a cobra. They were quick and powerful. Like the great athletes of today."

White met another legend when Adolph Rupp, the ultra-successful basketball coach at Kentucky, came down to speak in Tuscaloosa to football and basketball coaches in the state. White remembers that Rupp and Bryant had a rivalry at Kentucky when Bryant was the football coach there. Bryant did not like taking a backseat to basketball —but that was the way it was at Kentucky. That explains why Bryant took the job at Texas A&M—to get to a school where football was number one.

But Bryant wanted to strike a truce with Rupp so he had him down to Tuscaloosa. Rupp was happy to accept the invitation and smooth the waters, so to speak.

"He was confident in everything he said," White remembers. "Rupp really could get his message across. He was very impressive. Coach Bryant didn't want ill feelings. Coach Bryant introduced him. I introduced Paterno—that took some homework."

White recalls the 1979 Sugar Bowl against Penn State where he once suggested to Bryant to run the triple option; Jeff Rutledge could usually either run it or pitch the ball to Tony Nathan. Penn State ran a defense that Alabama expected so Rutledge called an audible at the line of scrimmage for the play to go to the weak side. Nathan didn't hear the audible because of the noise in the Superdome and made a step right instead of left. After faking the ball to the fullback, Rutledge ran to the left side of the line. As he was about to be hit by a defender, he pitched the ball, but Nathan wasn't there. Penn State recovered the fumble, which set up the final drive when Alabama made their famous goal-line stand when Barry Krauss, Marty Lyons, Murray Legg and company stood up Penn State running back Mike Guman on fourth and one.

"I was responsible for the goal-line stand," White says, kiddingly.

Speaking of suggestions, one of the most underrated duties during an assistant coach's nonstop year is recruiting. White had the north Alabama area to recruit and brought in plenty of winning football players. Thomas Boyd was one of them. Boyd was looking at Alabama and came down for a visit. Boyd was driving down with a friend and White called a florist friend in Huntsville to follow him down to the Tuscaloosa County line. White wanted to make sure Boyd made it down to Tuscaloosa. He did and later signed.

Hardy Walker was another prospect White recruited, thinking he could be another John Hannah. Walker was more of an intellectual and didn't respond well to the hollering of the coaches. White told the coaches that they couldn't talk to him the same way as they did some other players, but they didn't listen. Walker tore up a knee later in his career and never reached his potential, which White believed was unlimited.

Dale McMillan was another potential standout whom White recruited, but he got involved in a boating accident his sophomore year and broke his neck. He would have been a starting offensive lineman.

Sammy Hood was another. A quarterback and defensive back at Sand Mountain, Sammy was fast and aggressive and would make a great defensive back. White remembers sitting on the porch with his parents and rocking in rocking chairs. "They were as nice as could be." White showed Louis Campbell, the secondary coach, game film on Hood. White told Campbell, "Hood could run and he would hit you on defense." White showed Campbell film when Hood took on a big back and drilled him. Campbell turned off the film and said, "We'll take him." But Hood tore up his leg in an auto accident and never reached his potential.

"That was the best class I recruited ['80]. How could so many things go wrong?"

White had recruited other standouts earlier; Warren Lyles and

Jackie Cline were a couple. Hardy Walker and Willard Scissum were two players White recruited who were both heavyweight wrestlers and good ones, the best two in the state. Scissum beat Walker during their senior year. Walker had won the state in the heavyweight class his junior year.

White was great friends with Donahue and Paul Crane on the staff, but, "I respected them all."

Bill Oliver was secondary coach. "He was one of the best if not the best in the country." Mal Moore, now Athletics Director at the University, was the offensive coordinator. Dee Powell was offensive line coach and Bobby Marks coached the receivers. John Mitchell coached the tight ends. Jack Rutledge coached the centers and Dude Hennessey the defensive ends.

White had another coach he was close to outside of football. Don Gambril, who coached the swim team to major success, was a great friend. Gambril won SEC championships in both men's and women's divisions and coached the 1984 U.S. Olympic team. Gambril was inducted into the Alabama Sports Hall of Fame in 1998.

White has toured the Alabama Sports Hall of Fame in Birmingham, considered one of the best in the country. Athletes like Jesse Owens, Hank Aaron and Joe Louis have been inducted. White likes that Joe Louis gave the shortest acceptance speech ever given. Louis said, "I love Alabama and appreciate this award." Then he sat down.

White remembers a special back who played for him, John David Crowe. Tony Nathan was playing halfback against Notre Dame and Mal Moore was afraid to run the option because Nathan couldn't block the defensive end. White went up to Bryant and said Crowe could block him. Bryant told him to put Crowe in. White told Crowe "to put that kid on the ground or I'll get fired." Moore called the option to the left side and Crowe was supposed to block the end. "J. D. put him on the ground and Jack O'Rear, the quarterback, scored a touchdown. My contract was good for one more year."

Crowe died tragically some years later when his car lost a hubcap on the highway and as he was going out to pick it up he was hit by a car and killed instantly. "He was such a good kid. What a waste."

One of White's colleagues at the University was Clem Gryska. Gryska remembers White as much for his high school coaching prowess as for White's stint at Alabama, though he has fond memories of his friendship with White at the University. "He is a super guy, great sense of humor."

Gryska was the recruiting coordinator at Alabama; he used to visit Banks and was impressed by the way White never took his mind off his team even when there was a college coach at practice.

"We'd get to Banks about 2-2:30 p.m. and watch practice. Nothing would disrupt his practice. He would talk to us after and he'd be a different guy. But during practice he was focused on his team. When we went to Eufaula or Phenix City the coach would get away from a passing game drill and come talk to us about a particular player. But Shorty wouldn't do that."

Gryska says that White was a "precise" coach whose attention to detail was "rare." Gryska notes he was like that at Alabama when he was coaching running backs. White would run a drill and if a running back was not in the right stance, they would run the drill again until he got it right.

Gryska says that White was "a super coach, and a great person beyond that."

In the opinion of most sports fans in the Birmingham area, Clyde Bolton is a super writer. Bolton has distinguished himself by writing features, covering games and writing columns for *The Birmingham News* for 40 years. He also has written 17 books and still has the motor running in that business.

He and White have been good friends since their association at Alabama when White was an assistant in Tuscaloosa.

"I knew Shorty as a person of good cheer and a good sense of humor," Bolton says. "He was fun to talk to and he was obviously a great high school football coach. Shorty was one of the top five high school coaches I ever knew anywhere."

Bolton says that what was amazing about White was that you would never know he was a hard-nosed football coach if you spent time with him outside the arena.

"If you saw him at the grocery store you would never guess he was a great football coach. He would always be laughing or telling a story. He was always a good guy. You didn't see that tough demeanor outside of his job. But he was obviously great at what he did. When I covered Alabama he was always one of my favorite assistants."

Another one of Shorty's best friends on the staff was Jack Rutledge (no relation to Gary and Jeff's father) who coached with White at Alabama when White was there from '75-'81. Rutledge remembers White as a dedicated, cutting-edge coach who stayed on top of his profession and taught technique to perfection.

Rutledge played on Bear Bryant's first national championship team in '61 and was part of a coaching staff that won national championships at Alabama in '78 and '79.

"It takes three years to build a championship program," he asserts. "I think we laid the groundwork in '76 and '77 for the championship teams."

Rutledge remembers White as the consummate preparer for football players.

"He was so up to date on making adjustments and teaching technique. He was organized. He excelled at teaching players technique, especially blocking out of the backfield, how you got your head in there and the body lean, and turning your shoulder into your man."

Rutledge also knows White as a man you could trust.

"You could always depend on what Coach White said he was going to do. He was always on top of everything.

"Shorty took a little time adjusting as an assistant because he had always been a head coach. He had to adjust to other people's ideas. But what he taught could win today. You also couldn't find a better person than Coach White."

Rutledge says that he and White still discuss football today when they eat lunch in the "A" Club before Alabama games.

"He still talks about his philosophies. What he did is still in place today."

CHAPTER 17
Pleasant Grove (1991-1994)

After spending ten years in the business world, White coached at Pleasant Grove from '91-'94 and didn't have the kind of environment he experienced at Banks. There was simply not the commitment among the players that characterized all the Banks teams that White coached.

White recalls kids who were pampered and not disciplined at home and didn't dedicate themselves to an off-season program or conditioning during a season. White wasn't used to that. "They were not all that way. They deserve more from the other players." Four players received scholarships off Pleasant Grove teams under White.

At Banks the players were all middle class, hard-working kids whom Jeff Rutledge says would work jobs in the summer from 8-5, then go out to conditioning work for White after that. Banks boys were committed to excellence and the results spoke to that commitment. Pleasant Grove was different. White had kids who didn't want to work and an administration that didn't support him. It's different today as Pleasant Grove has kids who are committed and have been to the state playoffs on many occasions in the past ten years. But in the early '90s, White didn't get that type of attitude from those players that he expected, and showed himself, every day. It was a very frustrating experience for a coach who was used to the success that came through hard work and respect for one's head coach. That didn't happen.

"Pleasant Grove was a baseball community; they were very successful and had a nice feeder program," White says. "There was not much interest in football. The kids were undisciplined in the off-season. Any way they could get out of weight training they would. They'd always have an excuse."

White was not one to say football was all that mattered. He wanted his kids to play other sports—remember, he coached basketball, baseball, wrestling and track at Banks. He felt playing other sports kept his kids competitive.

"Things have changed there," White says. "They are now big, fast and hungry. Those guys fight for it today. Back then they were not willing to pay the price. That is just my opinion, seen through my eyes."

White, a great judge of character, is probably right.

White had a losing record at Pleasant Grove, something he wasn't used to. Shorty says he learned a lot from the experience even though he learned the hard way.

"Coaches and players learn more from defeat than they do winning. I think back on the losses we had and saw how I could have done things differently. And I think if I would have done some things differently, yes, I would have had a different outcome."

White's fear of losing drove him. Many of the great coaches concur. I remember Jimmy Johnson, who won the national championship at Miami and two Super Bowls with the Dallas Cowboys in the early '90s admitting the same fear.

" I think it goes back to my family life when I was young," White speculates. "My parents divorced, we didn't live in the neighborhood we'd have liked to live in, we wanted certain foods that we couldn't afford. When you get the opportunity to succeed you don't want to let it go and you work that much harder and you're much tougher."

I asked White about his status with other people. Some people didn't like him and were against him, something many successful coaches experience. There are always people trying to knock you off.

"Jack Rutledge, Jeff's dad, would always let me know, 'Throw the ball Shorty!' He'd get so upset. He even challenged Coach Bryant on the field one time. He was so upset when we lost a ball game against Georgia and Coach Bryant had the coaches in the office that Sunday morning about 5 a.m. and the players on the field at 6 a.m. The quarterbacks all got hurt in that practice and Jeff hurt his wrist. Jack went after Bear, who just kept walking. Jack was a religious guy, a deacon in the Baptist Church but he had a temper. Coach Bryant just walked away.

"Jack would get on me and I'd retort 'Jack how many points do you want us to score? We scored 50 or 60 points.' He calmed down. He and I liked each other."

When White got to Alabama, Bryant told him that he would be recruiting North Alabama, which had over half the schools in the state. Bryant told White he didn't want him recruiting Birmingham—the hotbed for prospects in the state—because he didn't think the coaches liked him that much in the area.

"Hell, if you kicked my butt every year I wouldn't like it either!" Bryant informed White.

"I thought I got along with them pretty well," White says. "Anytime you're on top for three years ('72-'74), that's going to happen."

White actually had good coaching friends in Birmingham; all the coaches just wanted to beat him. He and Mutt Reynolds at Ramsay were close and he got along well with Tandy Geralds of Woodlawn and Ray Williams of West End. They were just not friends during the season. Coaches are wired to win. When they don't, they really don't like the man who beat them. But these coaches liked each other and had a genuine respect for each other away from the field. That is just the nature of competition.

White believed in running the football as much as passing, if not more. Jeff Rutledge was his first prolific passer. White believes today that defensive coordinators are figuring out ways to stop the passing game, and while there are superstars like Peyton Manning who may not be able to be stopped, he believes the running game is critical to winning and that it is coming back into vogue.

"He is great at reading defenses and reading the secondary," Shorty says of Manning. "He's what a professional quarterback should be. But you've got to have a strong running game and you've got to have some luck."

White looks back on his decision to go to Alabama in '75 and he's not sure he wouldn't have liked to stay in Birmingham. He could have coached anywhere in the city and county with his name and resumé. And he loved city football. Banks' enrollment was going down, but football in the city was great with West End, Ramsay, Woodlawn, Ensley, Phillips and Huffman. "Everybody had good talent," White says. "It made competition so keen."

White looks back and knows he sent three children through college because of his coaching at the University and he played a role in two national championships. It was a meaningful and worthwhile experience for him. But White says the coaching and emphasis on all sports in the city made him love being in Birmingham.

"Woodlawn had good football under Johnny Howell, Ensley had good baseball, West End had good baseball and track, Huffman under Phil English was one of the best-coached baseball teams in Birmingham history, and Ronnie Baynes excelled at Tallassee. Mutt Reynolds at Ramsay had those guys pumping that steel. The only thing favorable about college coaching is that I didn't have to teach any classes."

White says he "really wanted to go down there [to Tuscaloosa] and learn the difference between high school and college coaching."

He says that the defenses were more sophisticated in college but that his offense at Banks was just as good in terms of X's and O's. His triple option was cutting-edge football.

White would gain a lot of memories in his experience at Alabama as he moved to another chapter in his life and career.

CHAPTER 18
Reflections (1995-2007)

Today Shorty White is a spiritual man who doesn't hide his faith. His faith and his family are the two most important things in his life.

"When I was a kid growing up in elementary school, high school and college I really wasn't that active in church. But I could always feel the Lord in my life. He was watching over me in troubled times. I could feel his presence.

"As we grow older, smarter, more intelligent in worldly things, we come to terms with the most important things. After June and I got married we joined the First Ensley Highlands Methodist Church and that's where my faith really started to grow. I've been so thankful for that.

"It's a shame that in your youth you just don't have a grasp on life. If you live long enough you eventually come around. Youth is wasted on youth. A lot of young people don't put their values in the right place but the majority come around. When you get older you realize the most important things in life—faith and love.

"I had never been 100 percent fulfilled with my faith until I joined the Pelham First Baptist Church. Brother Mike Shaw is the pastor and he's a Banks High graduate. The whole staff, including the Sunday School teacher, Gary Henry, is the best I've ever had. Sam Nugent is the music director. Brother Mike has a great sense of humor. I get excited about going to church because he has a different message every week. He has me sitting on the edge of my seat. He has a great delivery. Paul Moore, his associate, along with the music have drilled into my brain the importance of my faith. I am a total believer. I read the Bible every day and a devotional. I am more knowledgeable about it. If the whole world could believe in the Lord there would be peace on Earth and goodwill toward men."

Mike Shaw has been the pastor at First Baptist Church of Pelham for the past 28 years and in the last three years has established a close relationship with Shorty.

Shaw says Shorty is content with his life in his later years.

"He's a devoted husband, father and grandfather," Shaw says. "When you get older you don't get to do the things you used to do, but he is content and happy in his faith. He's still a man's man, but he has a very strong faith."

Shaw played B team football for Banks in the '60s and gained the utmost respect and reverence for White.

"I was terrified of him in those days. He was very successful and he believed in discipline, hard work and team play. He made Johnny Musso a complete player. Johnny was a great athlete but Coach treated him like everybody else. Coach really believed in defense because if you couldn't score you couldn't win."

Today Shaw and White are close friends and confidants. "He's got a great heart, he would go out of his way to help anybody. He's got a tremendous faith in God. When he looks back on his life he had a great career. He won state championships and he influenced so many young people's lives. People ask me today what would happen if Hoover played Banks. I say that Hoover wouldn't make a first down."

"If we could restore youth to the players from the '65, '72, '73 or '74 teams, we would welcome a game with Hoover," White says.

Shaw adds that Banks was a great place and the football team was the ultimate team: White was all about winning the right way.

"He didn't teach dirty football. You would play whistle to whistle but he would never sweep anything under the rug. He didn't play that way and he won anyway. He was and is a man of absolute integrity. His wife is as great as he is. They are a joy to be around."

After spending many years on the job, Shorty and June have found financial security and a time in their lives where they can relax and be with their family.

"We wake up every day and it's like we're on a vacation. We wake up every day and do what we want to do. We are not financially wealthy but we live comfortably."

And he can spend more time on his passion, his grandchildren.

"My kids are in great shape. Darryl lives very nicely and takes great vacations. He goes skiing every year with the family. Dianne and Mike have good vacations. Gary doesn't want to go anywhere except Panama City. He likes the food down there.

"We lived in Tuscaloosa and I told June I wanted to move back to Birmingham to be closer to the kids and grandchildren. She didn't want to at first, but then when we did she said, 'Yeah, you're right.'

"We're five minutes from Dianne, 20 minutes from Darryl and 35 minutes from Gary. I've gotten to see my kids and grandchildren a lot more. I see Dianne about every day. I talk to or see Darryl twice a week and Gary calls almost every day.

"When I was working I wasn't there as much, it was kind of like I was on a mission. I owe so much to June. June hung tough with me. She is tougher than I am.

"I remember once during a game, we weren't doing so well and June was in the stands. There was a man behind her saying bad things about me. June stood up and told him, 'You're talking about my husband and I don't appreciate it so shut up.' That guy shut his mouth pretty quick."

White has no reservations in sharing his feelings for his eight grandchildren.

"They are my pride and joy. Three of them have become teenagers and like all teenagers they want independence and they can rebel. Jaymie, Charlie and Riley can get a little rambunctious. Charlie is a smart kid. He was elected senior class president of the student body at Hewitt-Trussville and is now at the University. Jaymie is doing well at Auburn and working hard to get her veterinarian degree. Riley is a good athlete and a good employee for his dad. I'm hoping and praying he'll be a good employer someday. Charlie is smart, but so is Gary, his dad. Gary in his last quarter in junior college made straight A's.

"June and I came from not much means and we're living comfortably."

They are very happy, and so are their kids.

Darryl White, Shorty White's younger son, says his dad's demeanor at home was much different than the demeanor the coach brought to the football field. His dad was devoted to his two sons and daughter and has helped them athletically and in life.

"All the players said I would hate to have him as my dad because he's so tough on us," Darryl recalls. "But he was not anything like that at home. He was tough at school, but he was always at my Little League events and helped me get in a baseball league that was very good. He led me athletically. I had an older brother, Gary, and I learned not to make the same mistakes that he did."

He remembers his father being home at meals. Of course on Friday nights in the fall he would get home very late and there was always a lot of work to be done on Saturdays and Sunday afternoons in preparation for the next week's game.

And Darryl says that he liked having a father who was a legend in high school football in Alabama.

"Some people growing up don't like being the son of a famous father," Darryl says. "But I actually felt a lot of security in it. He never put any extra pressure on me or anything like that."

And he confirms what his players all say, that Shorty was a coach highly focused on what he was doing and ahead of his time in what he was teaching his players.

"He was on the cutting edge with whatever was going on," he says. "He had everything down to a science, everything was exact from the quality of the uniforms to the locker room, which was absolutely immaculate. He was very good at organizing and analyzing what a program needed." And Darryl says that, beyond that, as a coach he was a master psychologist when it came to dealing with his players.

"He knew what a kid needed to hear. When he had the toughest players to deal with he knew how to handle them. If he needed to deal with them when they caused trouble he would warn them sternly and give them one chance. If they messed up again they were kicked off the team. He knew when to chew them out and when to put his arm around them. He was like Coach Bryant in that regard."

And Shorty's youngest son concurs with White's former assistant coaches and players who all talk about White's unyielding work ethic.

"I asked him where he learned that and he said he learned the value of hard work and discipline in the military. But there was something else inside of him. He could just figure out what was going on inside a kid's head."

And Darryl knows his dad was a genius at figuring out where a player needed to be positioned on the field.

"He was an expert at that. He would always be moving guys around. He would move a running back to wide receiver and the next thing you know the kid's got a scholarship to Alabama. When I was in high school I always wanted to be a quarterback at Alabama. I played running back. He told me I needed to be a wide receiver and a kick returner in college because I was too small for running back or quarterback. It turned out those were the only positions I could play."

Darryl went to Alabama and played those positions for Bryant.

His son also says that White was the ultimate motivator. His players just never wanted to let him down.

"There was a Little League football coach who kind of lost it in a game and he found out that my dad was at the game. He was upset that my dad had seen him do that. Everybody who played for him wanted his approval. They truly wanted to be patted on the back by him. The guys who played for him always wanted him to say that they were good players. As far as motivating people he knew how to do that."

And Darryl says his three sons, Riley, Ramsey and Reagan, and his daughter, Chaney, have a great relationship with their granddad.

"He's a blast. My kids love him to death. My oldest son, Riley, is a hurdler and my dad has worked with him. Dad has invested a lot of time and effort to help make Riley be the best he can be. And he comes to all my kids' sporting events, well, not all of them but a lot of them."

Darryl remembers as a 13-year old attending the classic Banks-Woodlawn game in November of '74 that pitted superstar Jeff Rutledge of Banks against superstar Tony Nathan of Woodlawn. Both teams were undefeated; the winner would make the playoffs and the loser would stay home, as the playoffs had far fewer slots than they do today. Today Class 6A takes 32 teams from around the state but in '74 there were only eight teams that qualified and so playoff spots were at a premium. This was the battle of the two best teams in the state at the mecca of football at the time, Legion Field. Woodlawn was an extremely physical team and Banks had their usual hard-working, solid football players headed by Rutledge.

"It was Tony Nathan versus Jeff Rutledge," Darryl remembers. "Coach Bryant came to the game and told my dad that his team was like a college football team. Dad didn't think we played very well. We just didn't realize how big it was. You looked up at the stands and it was packed from goal line to goal line."

And it was a classic, an 18-7 Banks win. Rutledge did his part while Nathan was held in check most of the game until he scored late on a long run.

Darryl notes that his dad is still involved in football and has a major impact on many kids, not only his own grandchildren.

"We run a Briarwood youth football camp and he's spent time with our seventh grade quarterback. The kid threw for 800 yards in 10 games and was phenomenal. Dad is an expert on how to throw the football, how to get the game down to a science and teach it and work it."

Darryl, like his dad's former players, is perplexed that his dad is not in the Alabama Sports Hall of Fame, when there is no doubt he should be in there.

"I don't know how you can spend 14 years somewhere, go 35 games in a row without a loss, win three state championships and not get in, it's a mystery to me," Darryl says. "There is no other coach that I've seen in 30 years of following the sport who is talked about the way my dad is talked about. Back then race was a factor but if you talk to Tony Nathan you'll know what he thinks about my dad."

Nathan was a huge fan of the Coach's. He still is to this day.

"He's had some of the best players to ever play high school write letters for him," Darryl says. "Jeff Rutledge, Billy Strickland (who played at Banks and started at Alabama) and Gary Rutledge (also a White disciple and an Alabama starting quarterback) —all have written letters for him. Anybody who knows about high school football is shocked."

But the coach is a bona fide legend in the state and will always be. Hopefully the Hall will realize that and induct him soon.

"I remember when my dad and I went around the state selling air purifiers, we'd go everywhere and there was more of 'You're Shorty White, I can remember when...' There were all kinds of stories."

The Coach created a lot of classic football memories, and his legend in Alabama football will always be remembered by many fans throughout the entire state. His election to the Hall of Fame should be a given. His son is one of many influential players who believe this should happen. Eighty-eight other players who earned college football scholarships along with his entire coaching staff and all of his players believe this should happen.

His daughter Dianne Barker is a huge advocate of this accolade. Shorty's only daughter was well protected by her father growing up even though, Dianne admits, she was a bit "feisty" as a youngster. She and her dad locked horns on occasion. It made for some pretty humorous episodes.

"I was kind of a smart aleck," Dianne laughs. "Dad would say something to me and I'd always say something back trying to get in the last word. He would chase me and I'd run in the bathroom and lock the door. One time he took the lock off the door and he got in. He was kind of grinning when he came in the door. He was kind of a jokester."

Dianne would also hide under the bed when she and her Dad got in an argument when she was little.

"I was under the bed one time and he acted like he got his head stuck under the bed. I came out from under the bed because I was worried about him and my adrenaline took over and I lifted the bed up. His head wasn't stuck. I cared about him a lot. He did funny stuff like that."

Dianne remembers her dad as a celebrity because of his legendary coaching ability. She knows that her dad was a strict disciplinarian at school and if the kids didn't act right he would be hard on them. But Dianne says that he was focused on what he was doing and was all about doing the right thing.

"He was very dedicated to not only his job but his players and his kids at school. He really cared about them. There were a lot of kids with financial problems who had their power turned off sometimes and he was a father figure to them. A lot of them today still call him and have a deep respect for him. He was always available to be a father figure and that is a great character trait."

Dianne says that her dad taught his players a lot more about life than just being good football players. He taught them about having character. "A lot of them are very successful today and he brought them up. A lot of them will tell you that."

Her dad was gone a lot and didn't have much time to spend with family, but today he is a great father and grandfather.

"He's just a big kid now. He missed out a lot on his childhood losing his parents at a young age. He was always at work. He had a lot of stress with his job. Now he's so easygoing and funny and he spends a lot of time with his grandkids."

Dianne and Mike Barker have two daughters, Brittney and Brooke. Brooke was the star of her basketball team when she was eight, sometimes scoring 20 points a game. Shorty was there for most of the games.

"He had to work hard to provide for the three kids and his wife. He had hard days but he loved his job. It required so much of his time. But I have no resentment because he was always helping other kids with their problems. We are close today and I'm closer now to my Mom than I was when I was younger."

Dianne calls her dad, "humble and friendly."

She says he has displayed impeccable character.

"He has always been of good character and is a real good friend. He is a very sound person and real likeable and outgoing. A lot of people like to be around him and admire him."

Dianne remembers that when her dad got the assistant coaching position at Alabama she was upset, because she wanted to stay at Banks for "selfish reasons. I was 15 and most 15-year-olds are selfish. At the same time I was proud that he was offered the opportunity to coach under Coach Bryant."

Dianne says she has a great relationship with her father today; he loves to talk about football to her and she tries to appease him by listening to him. "He still draws up plays. He's still so into football in general."

She says most of the students were afraid of her father.

"My dad would let me go out with only freshmen and sophomores when I was a freshman. One time a football player took me out and when we were walking to the door he heard my dad's voice and he ran away. He took off. It was kind of irritating."

Dianne says her dad has become very spiritual. He was baptized at Pelham Baptist Church and Johnny Musso came to town for it. Dianne says that was a "very special day. We spent all day with Johnny."

One time the minister of her church—this was before White joined the church—told the congregation about a coach he had had at Banks High School who'd made him do chin-ups. When he couldn't do a chin-up the coach paddled him. After the service Dianne asked the minister who the coach was and he said "Shorty White." "I told him that he is my dad."

Dianne is very proud of her father for what "a good man he was and is.

"He came up in a non-productive environment and he is an example that you don't have to be like that. He was a college football player, he got a college degree, a graduate degree, and a good job. A lot of people would use an alcoholic parent or a broken home as an excuse to fail. He didn't. He came out a winner."

She remembers her uncle, Jimmy Sidle and her dad as being very close. She was close to her uncle too, who lived with them for some years. "He and my dad always stayed close. It was really sad when he passed away."

Dianne is most proud of her father, and his most important accomplishment, coming from no means and making something substantial out of himself while positively touching so many lives.

Gary, the oldest, also has nothing but admiration and respect for his father.

Shorty was one of the tougher football coaches in the state at a time when tough coaches were the norm. Paddling was acceptable and not questioned by parents. Gary encountered this brand of discipline at home. When he got in trouble at school or made a bad grade there was going to be some harsh discipline employed at home. That was the way Gary's dad operated.

"He believed in discipline in everything he did," Gary says. "When I got in trouble at school it usually meant the belt. I don't know if you can discipline like that these days. Believe me, he got your attention."

But Shorty White was not only about disciplining his kids. He was also concerned about taking care of them.

"He was a good father. He provided everything we needed. He'd work extra to make sure we got what we needed and more than we needed. He wanted to make sure we had a better life growing up than he did."

Gary says that his dad was equally concerned about grades in school as he was with performance on the football field. "If you didn't pass, you didn't play and he had that standard for us and his football team."

Gary learned the value of the work ethic from his dad, a tireless worker.

"I don't think anybody worked harder on his profession than he did. He'd work in his office late reviewing films, meeting with his coaches and working with the Booster Club that provided the best uniforms, kept the field in top shape and kept an outstanding weight room. All were top notch."

White was a fair coach who played no favorites, particularly on the football field.

"I didn't get any favoritism," son Gary insists. "It was a little harder for me. Jeff Rutledge was a year ahead of me and I definitely did not play in front of him."

When Shorty White took the job at Alabama as an assistant in 1975, Gary remained at Banks and lived with his uncle in Birmingham, Jimmy Sidle.

"We had a terrible year in 1975. We had gone downhill pretty bad. A lot of seniors didn't come out for football."

Gary has been a business analyst for NCP Solutions involved in data processing for the company. He has been with NCP since 1989. He says his attention to detail, and drive to get things right, comes from his dad.

"I learned a good bit from him. He taught me about being dedicated to something. He was pretty much a perfectionist on the field. He would run a play over and over until we got it right. It's rubbed off on me at work. I spend a lot of time testing programs and I test every aspect of them. There is no room for error."

Gary says that his dad was all about being "a good citizen" off the football field too. Shorty White preached about being a good person in everything you do and that carried over into all aspects of Gary's life.

"He's been a terrific grandfather too," Gary brags of his dad, who has eight grandchildren: Gary and Cecelia have two children, daughter Jaymie and son Charlie; Dianne and Mike have two daughters, Brooke and Brittney; and Darryl and Janice have four children, sons Riley, Ramsey and Reagan and daughter Chaney.

"He's been supportive in anything they wanted to do. My daughter wants to be a vet and she's at Auburn and he's been very supportive of her. My son played football for a couple of years and it just wasn't for him. He is more into academics. My dad is real proud of his academics. Charlie has taken courses at Jeff State (a junior college outside Birmingham) and probably will be a sophomore in college when he enters school like my daughter was. He has never lost a debate and Samford is interested in him for a possible scholarship, as is Alabama for an academic scholarship. My dad has been very involved in that."

Gary also says that his dad goes to most football games that Darryl's sons play in and attends most of Dianne's daughters' dance functions or athletic events.

"He had a tough life growing up and he always wanted things to be better for us."

Gary often has someone who has a child Jaymie or Charlie's age say something about his dad, whether it be someone who taught at Banks or someone who knew about him. And younger boys will have dads who have told them about Shorty White.

"I couldn't be prouder to have a dad like I have. He always stayed focused. He's mellowed in his older years but he's always been focused on what he's doing. Now it's golf, going to his grandchildren's events or having a gathering with his old players for a reunion or a lunch."

To Gary, nobody was better at shaping the lives of the young people his father developed.

"He was able to take young kids and make something out of them. He encouraged them to strive to be their best. He did what he thought was expected. I never heard him brag on himself. It's hard to express what I feel about him. He was just a great father and a great coach. He was a true father figure to his players, sometimes more than they had at home. Some guys didn't have a father figure as home for one reason or another. He truly cared about his players."

Shorty is also devoted to his wife. June and Shorty White celebrated their 50th wedding anniversary in the summer of 2006. June has been a rock in Shorty's life. She retired from the Tuscaloosa City Board of Education in 1997, where she had worked as an administrative assistant for 22 years. In February of 2000, she and Shorty moved to Helena, presently called home. These are her thoughts on her marriage to the Coach:

"It's not the 50th anniversary that matters, it's the years in between that make up that 50 years. It's being together and still loving each other more now than ever. Sometimes I don't like him but I still love him. Sometimes he doesn't like me too. He's fun to be with and really keeps me laughing. Laughter is so good for your well-being.

"I would have never thought that we would become so alike. We are both homebodies and just enjoy each other's company. However I must say that I do like him to play golf as much as he can and he likes me to go shopping. My son Gary will call, and if he doesn't get an answer he leaves a message, 'I guess you're golfing and shopping' and he's usually right.

"At times when he was coaching it got lonely but I didn't know any different. That's the way of life for the wife of a coach. He left his problems at school. I made all but two of his games. One was when Dianne had an appendectomy and another was a Thursday night when both boys had games. We've had our good times and our bad times, mostly good times. George was a tough coach but he can be the sweetest person in the world. He's been a good husband and a good father. We couldn't have been together 50 years if he hadn't been. George is my best friend. We have been blessed with three great children and their wonderful spouses. They have given us eight grandchildren who we love and enjoy being with so very much."

A good husband, father and coach, of course White has some regrets about his career, but he has grown as a person and looks back at life with peace.

"If I had to do it all over again knowing what I know now, it would have been a lot better. I wanted to win so badly. I wanted to win too badly. My biggest disappointment was my last game at Banks, the '74 playoffs versus Homewood. We got beat by only 12 points, by a team that would win the state championship. My number one quarterback, Rutledge, was injured, I had injuries on the defensive side of the ball and my number two quarterback, Gary White, was in bed sick Monday, Tuesday and Wednesday. How do you play without a quarterback? I was down in the dumps. The kids gave me a lift. If we had been healthy all week we would have won. I went into the game in an emotional slump. I was down to 38 kids and no quarterback had taken a snap that week. One kid, Bob Grefseng, was playing with mono. I had two kids, Jerry Murphree and Jerry McDonald who I should have worked with in the spring at quarterback, like I had worked the spring before with Rick Neal before Jeff's junior year. The year before, Murphree had thrown a halfback pass for a touchdown against Grissom in our state championship win. I just took a risk that Jeff would stay healthy."

When White started out in 1961 as head football coach, Banks was inferior in talent to Woodlawn, Ramsay, Ensley and sometimes even Jones Valley. They were on par with Phillips and West End. White built a dynasty and his state championships in '65, '72 and '73 attest to that. But the losses stuck with him. Though they hurt, he gained a lot of wisdom from them.

"I've learned more from losing than winning. I learned a lot from that last loss at Banks. I didn't give those kids a chance. I didn't motivate them. There was a complete drop-off in morale. It's not what I said, it's what I didn't say. I was so proud of our defense. They played well enough to win. Anytime you can hold your opponent to 12 points you should win." And with the way the Banks offense had been scoring that year it should have been good enough. But the team was depleted.

"I don't care what profession you're in, the older you get—if you have a brain at all—you become smarter and you make better decisions. You think before you react. I could have taken Murphree or McDonald and put them in at quarterback in the spring. It was not their fault, it was mine. I lost the game and boy, that hurts.

"Nobody is going to win 'em all. If you coach and play long enough, you're going to get whipped. The other team can have better material and the other coach can outcoach you. The coaches in Birmingham were all good and they wanted to win as much as I did.

"At the beginning of the season I told my team that there was going to be a game where we won't play as well as we're capable of and the other team will get ahead of us. I told them we'll find out what kind of football team we have when we have to come from behind."

It was a great career with some regrets, but it featured one constant: June.

"She has been so supportive through the good times and the bad times. I couldn't have picked a better soul mate. She has been so good for me. She's helped me grow up. We've had some rough spots but we've always managed to work through them. She's been with me and will be with me till death do us part."

CONCLUSION

When I first met Coach Shorty White in 1991 he was the head football coach at Pleasant Grove. I was working for *The Birmingham News* and I always got to games about an hour early to talk to the coaches and get their insights as to what it would take to win the football game.

I was so impressed with the way Shorty handled my questions and how focused and calm he was before a game. I came away thinking how professional he was, how likeable a man he was. His team didn't win the game—they played a very strong Midfield team and lost, in a highly competitive contest. Yet there is no doubt Coach is a competitor and a champion, superb at preparing his teams to compete. His three state championships at Banks are a testament to that. He should have had four at least, and would surely have achieved that fourth had Jeff Rutledge not broken his ankle in the last game of the '74 regular season.

But the main thing about Coach—he is a great guy. He likes people and he cultivates relationships. He was very fond of the writers in the '60s and '70s at *The Birmingham News*, pros like Wayne Martin, Ronald Weathers, Herbie Kirby and Clyde Bolton. They were positive guys who reported facts without inserting their opinion in stories. Opinions should be limited to columns where one can blast somebody or compliment a great achievement or demonstration of great character. There is too much opinion today in sportswriting and not enough reporting.

Granted there is a lot that is not right about sports today. There are major egos who need to be humbled and brought back to Earth, instead of luxuriating in their egocentric worlds. Pro sports is full of that.

But there is also a major ego problem among sports radio guys and some writers. Talk radio is full of guys who say some irresponsible things. There is a lot of negative out there with steroids, DUI's, handguns, theft of property and abuse of women, but there is also a reporting of "facts" that aren't true. The stories are written so a writer can put his name out there, to become famous.

I do like a lot of sportswriters and broadcasters. But I hear a lot of these play-by-play guys on football, basketball or baseball injecting their opinions, when that is the point of having an analyst. You don't want to hear that; it gets in the way of the game. A true professional, be he a good waiter at a restaurant, a good judge in the courtroom, a good official on the field or a good writer or broadcaster, stays out of the way. In the sports arena, let the athletes and the coaches provide the drama of the game: the players with their play on the field and the coaches with their decision-making on the sidelines. In other words, report the facts. Kirk Herbstreit is a great commentator as is Todd Blackledge. They are the guys who need to be asserting their opinions, not the play-by-play guys though they do have an opinion and can inject their opinions at certain times. Keith Jackson was always good about calling the game, making some insightful observations and letting his sidekick do the job of dissecting the majority of the game. Herbstreit and Blackledge both played the game and they are the ones who should express their opinions for the most part.

I like Sean McDonough who calls college football for ESPN among other sports. He does inject some opinion but it doesn't come across as abrasive or too opinionated and he calls a great game.

Jim Rome is good and interesting, but there are guys out there with their own agendas and I think even Rome, though I do agree with most of what he has to say, can cross the line at times in his criticism.

I love sports and love the banter. I don't like seeing a guy causing or getting in trouble. It has to be reported on and I'm not that Pollyannish to where I think athletes are all good people. Some of them are not and some get in trouble.

I would just like to see better things ahead in sports. I like talk radio, but I don't love it. I like the work of a lot of columnists. Analyzing sports is a great profession.

There is a lot wrong with athletics today with professional athletes' personal lives and decisions. I think too many of the young guys are so wrapped up in making tons of money that they are not realistic about their own skills. The best example is in basketball, where these young kids come out for the NBA when they should go to college for at least two years and learn skills and become better players. It has hurt the level of play, using these kids who aren't ready; the kids don't make it and what have they got left? They can play in Europe obviously and make a decent living, but their dream is destroyed because they were unduly influenced and became overly impatient. Gain some skills, get better at the game and try to get a college degree! Basketball is over for many of these guys when they get to their mid-30's and what do they have left? Granted they've got money and they don't have to work, but what kind of life is that? Golf all the time gets old.

There needs to be more responsibility in sports, not only in the way it is reported, but also in the way these agents and athletes conduct themselves.

Sports is great, it always will be, but it can get a lot better if individuals would act like professionals and not let their egos get in the way of doing a job the right way and making smart decisions that they've put thought into. That probably applies to society as a whole.

Shorty White did not hesitate to do the right thing. He has lived his life with integrity, toughness, compassion, desire, and devotion to his family and the players fortunate enough to have played for him. He passed on critical life skills to his players who became highly successful in their own right, and they in turn were equipped to pass on moral values to their children. Shorty is a principled man who has done things "the right way." All of us can learn from this man's life: his legacy remains proven values that last throughout generations. George "Shorty" White is a man of honor, compassion, and kindness; my respect for him is everlasting. He should occupy an honored place in Alabama sports history.

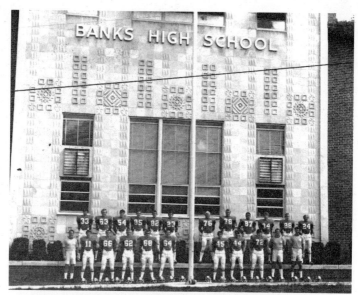

1972 Banks High School State Champions

Coach

Banks High School Staff (from left) Mike Foster, Dyer Carlisle and Mike Dutton Coach (kneeling)

1973 Banks High School State Champions

Jeff Rutledge

Jerry Murphree

Bob Grefseng

Freddie Knighton

Jerry McDonald

Coach and Freddie Knighton

Coach

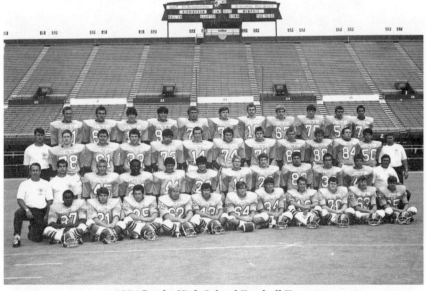

1974 Banks High School Football Team

1965 State Championship Team with Auburn Head Football Coach Ralph "Shug" Jordan (top row from left) Jordan, Jeff Masters, Ronnie Massey, Johnny Musso, Larry Willingham, Larry Gunnin, and Coach (bottom row from left) Allan Girardeau, Sam Chambliss, Johnny Johnston, Billy Strickland, and Merrill Mann

Coach at 1965 State Championship Address (standing from left) Bill Lankford, Bill Burgess, Don Green, Billy Strickland, Johnny Johnston, and Allan Girardeau

Photo Courtesy of the *Birmingham Post-Herald*

Jerry Murphree Running Behind Blocking of Bob Grefseng

Photo Courtesy of *The Birmingham News*

"Johnny Musso Takes a Dive"

Photo Courtesy of *The Birmingham News*

Photo Courtesy of the *Birmingham Post-Herald*

Coach

Jeff Rutledge

Photo Courtesy of the *Birmingham Post-Herald*

Jeff Rutledge

Photo Courtesy of the *Birmingham Post-Herald*

*Coach (right) at Birmingham Touchdown Club Working Coaches Golf Tournament
(from left) Mal Moore, J.D. Ferguson, and Fred Stephens*

Coach with Major Ogilvie

Jimmy Sidle Sports Illustrated *Cover*

ACKNOWLEDGMENTS

I'd like to thank the people who were so inspirational and critical to this project.

First of all I'd like to thank my editor and good friend John T. Bird. John is an accomplished author, having written the acclaimed *Twin Killing: The Bill Mazeroski Story*, about Pittsburgh Pirate great Bill Mazeroski. John's book was so compelling to readers in the greater Pittsburgh area and around the country that he helped get Mazeroski elected to the Baseball Hall of Fame. John was dedicated and tireless in his efforts to get this project completed on time and his editing was precise and impeccable. John you're a pro and a great friend. Your keen knowledge of the language and your expertise in sports was invaluable to the project. Thank you so much.

Melanie McCraney was a major player in my first book, *Leadership Lessons for Life*, and was her usual dedicated, hard-working public relations point person for the book. Melanie you are an incredible marketer and your energy and enthusiasm for the book is so appreciated and I respect your work immensely.

I want to also thank my designer, Bill Segrest. Bill, you were invaluable in my first book as well and you are the consummate professional who goes above the call of duty in your work. You produced a terrific product in a short period of time. You're the best and I appreciate your efforts in putting out a first-class design while also working full time as an architect. Your efforts were superior.

June White, the first lady of the Coach, was so kind and hospitable to me throughout the interviews with Coach. June you are a great lady and as they say, "behind every great man there is a great woman." There is no doubt you are that. Thanks so much for your lunches and your kind and giving nature.

Lastly, I want to thank my wonderful wife, Beth. Beth, without you I don't know what I would do. Your help in this project was immeasurable. Your encouragement throughout the process kept me going. As the late greats, Marvin Gaye and Tammi Terrell sang, "Ain't no mountain high enough ... to keep me from gettin to you." You and the girls are all I need.